Dearest C... be

This is

a very

Hope you g...

Love, Antoinette,

D0421862

THE FRIDGE-HIKER'S GUIDE TO LIFE

THE FRIDGE-HIKER'S GUIDE TO LIFE

How to Stay Cool When You're Feeling the Heat

TONY HAWKS

EBURY
PRESS

1 3 5 7 9 10 8 6 4 2

Published in 2008 by Ebury Press, an imprint of Ebury Publishing
A Random House Group Company

Copyright © Tony Hawks 2008

Tony Hawks has asserted his right to be identified as the author
of this Work in accordance with the Copyright, Designs and
Patents Act 1988

Illustrations © Peter Mac, www.petermac.com

All rights reserved. No part of this publication may be
reproduced, stored in a retrieval system, or transmitted in any
form or by any means, electronic, mechanical, photocopying,
recording or otherwise, without the prior permission of the
copyright owner

The Random House Group Limited Reg. No. 954009

Addresses for companies within the Random House Group
can be found at www.randomhouse.co.uk

A CIP catalogue record for this book is available from
the British Library

The Random House Group Limited supports The Forest
Stewardship Council (FSC), the leading international forest
certification organisation. All our titles that are printed on
Greenpeace approved FSC certified paper carry the FSC logo.
Our paper procurement policy can be found at
www.rbooks.co.uk/environment

Mixed Sources
Product group from well-managed
forests and other controlled sources
www.fsc.org Cert no. TT-COC-2139
© 1996 Forest Stewardship Council

FSC

ISBN 9780091924188

To buy books by your favourite authors and register for offers
visit www.rbooks.co.uk

Printed and bound in Germany by
GGP Media GmbH, Pössneck

CONTENTS

AUTHOR'S NOTE

In February 2007 I made a short tour of Australia where I gave several talks about my first book, *Round Ireland with a Fridge*, and what I'd learned from the adventures therein. I was surprised to find that people were coming up to me after these events and telling me how helpful and applicable to their own lives they'd found the 'lessons' that lay within the various stories. An equally surprising number of people even urged me to try and write a book that might set it all out in a lucid and simple way. I hope I have succeeded with the book you now hold in your hands.

I shall be donating all of the royalties I receive from this book to charities consistent with the themes outlined within it (details at www.thefridgetrust.com).

Tony Hawks, May 2008
www.tony-hawks.com

PROLOGUE

Life, love and the universe are big things. Especially the universe. This is generally accepted by everyone. Protestants, Catholics, Jews, Muslims, atheists, agnostics and the rest may differ on a fair amount of stuff, but on the size of the universe we're all pretty much as one. It's big. There are people who will tell you the star you're looking at in the night sky is so many millions of light years away that it's actually not there any more. How these people come up with this stuff I'm not sure, but some of them have lots of letters after their names so they must know what they're talking about. According to them, the star exploded a while back and what you're looking when you 'see' the star is the light it once emitted, which has taken millions of years to reach you. In the meantime, the star has buggered off – so when you 'see' the star, you're looking at something that isn't there.

Now for those of us who consider the walk to the shops a bit of a long way, this is just 'big'ness gone mad. For those of us who like a simple life where we can pretty much understand everything that's going on around us, someone telling us we're looking at something that isn't there means they're either:

a) showing off,
b) drunk,
c) much cleverer than us,

or

d) all of the above.

If you've already divined from the tone of this prologue that this book isn't going to be packed full of astronomical facts or scientific detail, then you've done well. If, like me, your head begins to hurt when you have to think about the concept of looking at something that isn't there, then you can rest assured that this little book will not test you any further in this domain. I would simply ask you to accept that there's not only some stuff we don't know, there's probably also a whole load more that we can't comprehend.

The Fridge-Hiker's Guide isn't really going to tackle this.

It won't attempt to answer the big mysteries of life, like: 'Where did we come from?' 'Where do we go?' or 'Why do "inflammable" and "flammable" mean exactly the same thing?' A lot of brilliant minds have attempted to sort this stuff out and, frankly, all they've really managed to do is to agree to disagree. (Sometimes they haven't even agreed on that.) I won't deny that the various thinkers who have engaged in this activity are much cleverer than I am. I would argue, however, that my conspicuous lack of intellectual sophistication and brain power has enabled me to stumble upon some very simple truths that require little more than common sense in order for them to make life an enjoyable experience.

Try this, for example:

All you have between birth and death is a journey
— and if the journey is all we have, then wouldn't
it be best to make it fun?

We don't need to overcomplicate this.

DOING SOMETHING A BIT SILLY

In May 1997 I hitch-hiked round the circumference of Ireland with a small refrigerator in order to win a hundred-pound bet. It was a very eccentric thing to do. The reason I ended up doing it was because I'd seen the 'Fridge Man' years before.

Let me explain.

On the first trip I'd ever made to Ireland I'd been picked up at Dublin airport by an Irish driver who was taking me to a place called Cavan. About half an hour out of the city, just as dusk was falling, I saw something extraordinary by the side of the road. An old boy was hitching with a bloody great refrigerator beside him. I was stunned. I turned to my driver:

'Was that man hitching with a fridge?'

'Oh yeah.'

And that was it. Nothing else from the driver. No visible sign of any surprise.

I was amazed, not just by the sight of the venerable old hitch-hiker, but by the fact that the fridge-hitcher's presence by the roadside had failed to provoke any kind of notable reaction from my Irish driver. I deduced that we were in a country where one had to do a good deal more than hitch by the side of the road with a fridge to qualify as eccentric. What did you have to do in these parts, I wondered, to become a conversation point?

Years later, I told this story at a dinner party and, after a good deal of wine had flowed, I ended up making a rather bold statement:

'Ireland is the one place in the world where you could hitch-hike with a fridge.'

The assertion was questioned. Naturally enough, I defended it. Soon I was locked in a pointless dispute with my friend Kevin as to whether Ireland was a country where you could easily hitch-hike with a refrigerator. It seemed like there was only one sensible way to resolve things.

And so it was that in the morning I woke up with a monster hangover, and a note pinned to my bedroom door.

I HEREBY BET TONY HAWKS THAT HE
CANNOT HITCH-HIKE AROUND THE CIRCUM-
FERENCE OF IRELAND WITH A FRIDGE
WITHIN ONE CALENDAR MONTH.

And below these words was Kevin's signature, and underneath that an unintelligible squiggle that I took to be mine.

And so the bet was made.

Now, it's no good me pretending that the gauntlet had been thrown down and that my honour was at stake if I didn't pick it up and rise to the challenge set before me. I had been drunk and so had Kevin, and if people were held to things said when sloshed, then we'd all be tragic heroes, ensnared in miserable lives forced upon us by our own reckless words. I'd still be with Alison Wilcox, whom I'd told I would 'love forever' in the midst of a lager-sodden teenage one-night stand. I find it difficult to imagine us still together now – mortgage, kids and Ford Mondeo – given that the only thing we had in common in the morning was mutual embarrassment.

In fact, when I did get round to calling Kevin, he had only a very sketchy recollection of the whole thing. He was hardly going to hold me to something he could barely remember himself. So why, a month later, did I find myself seriously considering taking the bet on? There was no need, no need at all, and yet there I was looking at a map of Ireland and trying to work out the mileage involved in making its coastal circuit. Alas, I had been struck down with what psychoanalysts refer to as GTDSBS syndrome.*

Naturally, the adopted logic of those suffering from GTDSBS syndrome is flawed and can be easily exposed. I cite a short conversation I had with a mountaineer (mountaineers are probably the most common casualties of this phenomenon) as an example of how easily this may be achieved: 'Why, in the bitter conditions of an Alpine winter, are you tackling the dangerous and challenging north-eastern face of the fearsome Matterhorn?'

'Because it's there.'

'But so are your slippers and the TV remote.' QED, I think.

And yet I was just as deluded as the mountaineer, maybe even more so. All logic defied what I found myself contemplating. I would sit up late at night weighing up the pros and cons. All right, the cons won

* Going To Do Something a Bit Silly syndrome

hands down, but there were times when I managed to make the whole thing seem glamorous. An adventure, the unknown, the chance to do something no one had done before. Wow! Something no one had done before. Most of us can only dream of that.

If you're not sure of the lengths to which people are prepared to go in order to set themselves apart from their fellow man, then have a browse through *The Guinness Book of Records* next time you find yourself with a couple of free minutes in the reference library.

That's exactly what I found myself doing one morning – checking the entries under Refrigerators and Hitch-hiking, just to confirm that the whole Ireland/fridge venture hadn't already been successfully undertaken by a seventeen-year-old biology student from Sheffield. Research brought relief when I discovered that nobody had done it.

To my surprise, this bet with Kevin refused to become something I could put down to a moment of drunken madness and leave be. However much I tried to forget about it, I kept waking up in the middle of the night thinking about fridges, and dreaming about hitching with one. A nagging little voice within me just wouldn't shut up.

History is full of cases where people seem to receive some kind of 'calling'. Usually it's for some magnificent cause – to lead a downtrodden people to freedom, to overturn an unjust and oppressive law, or to reach some uncharted and distant point on earth for the first time. Was it some kind of cruel joke that my calling appeared to be that I should hitch-hike round the circumference of Ireland with a small fridge?

The nagging little voice within. The gut feeling. We all have it, nudging us in a direction, urging us to do something or causing us to have misgivings about something we're about to do. But how often do we ignore it, or persuade ourselves it's just a silly voice?

All I can say is that if I'd ignored this particular gut feeling, then I would have missed out on a pretty amazing journey that has allowed my life to change direction. If I hadn't listened to the little voice inside nagging at me to honour my drunken bet, then I wouldn't have profited from a very special experience. So perhaps the first thing I learned from my adventure happened before I even set off:

Find the courage to follow your intuition.

A month after I'd found the courage to follow my intuition, I found something else as well.

I found myself on a stretch of bleak Irish roadside in the pouring rain, fridge and rucksack at my feet.

Eek!

The odyssey had begun.

'I'M JUST PARKING HERE'

I hauled my load slowly to a suitable spot on the road-side, noticing with some concern that cars were coming by at alarmingly irregular intervals. In a physical and emotional state close to numbness, I arranged myself by the road and tried to force myself to feel optimistic. Although the rain had eased off, it was still spitting and the clouds on the horizon suggested that it wouldn't be long before the waterproofs would have to come out. I surveyed the surroundings with which I hoped I wouldn't become too familiar and saw that I had chosen a bleak, unwelcoming stretch of road on which to begin my journey. It wasn't ugly and it certainly wasn't attractive; it was just a dull stretch of Irish road. Electricity pylons, a couple of fields and the back view of a sign pointing the other way which, with any luck, read 'NO SCOFFING AT THE HITCHER'. I put the fridge a little way in front of me and leant the rucksack against it, trying to create an impression of normality – that a fridge, a trolley and a rucksack *should* be seen together – and I stuck my thumb out.

A Ford Fiesta sped past. Then a Vauxhall Cavalier. A Renault next, and then a red car whose make I couldn't fathom. That was four cars and none of them had shown any sign of stopping. What was going wrong? Had they not seen that my thumb was out? Were they not intrigued by the sight of this fridge? A Citroen, a large truck, a Ford Escort and a BMW later, I sat on the fridge and consulted my watch. Eight vehicles had been past and I had been there eight minutes. This was only a car a minute. I checked the second hand, and waited another minute. Oh dear. Nothing. Things were going from bad to worse. Even less than one car a minute. I tried to escape from this statistical mire by giving myself a pep talk in which I resolved to think positively for a quarter of an hour or so. I got up off the fridge and attempted to stand in such a way as to present myself as a strong, positive man with nonetheless an air of vulnerability about him, thinking that this might give me the best 'across the board' appeal to oncoming drivers.

This gave me cramp. So I sat back down on the fridge and wondered how I could have been so naive as to expect a steady flow of traffic on a main road. Maybe I should have a piece of card with my destination written on it. Maybe I should have got a card and written 'ANYWHERE' on it. Maybe I should have recognised the difference between a funny idea and the practicality of attempting to act it out. Cars passed with an infrequency that left me having fantasies about traffic congestion. The numbness I had felt when I began had long since disappeared and instead I now found my emotions lurching from one extreme to the other. Each time I could see a car or truck on the horizon I would become filled with expectation. 'This is it! This is the one!' As it drew nearer I would allow my hopes to rise to such an extent that when it sped by I felt bitterly rejected.

Twenty minutes and seventeen bitter rejections later, I was beginning to feel a little low. Three or four weeks of this kind of torment would leave me in need of expensive counselling. My thoughts turned to the bet. I could handle losing a hundred pounds, and the knock to the pride would be considerably less than a daily dose of what I was having to suffer now.

Contemplating giving up after less than half an hour was not the start I had envisaged. No doubt about it, I was on the ropes. Actually I was on the canvas with the count having reached about six.

Occasionally a couple would go by and I could see what looked like the beginning of a conversation starting between them.

'Was that a fridge?'

'What?'

'That guy back there – hitching – did he have a fridge with him?'

'You're tired, darling. Stop in a minute and I'll take over driving.'

Don't talk about it, I thought. Stop and pick the poor bugger up! Self-centred bastards, you had room in your car.

Never again was *I* going to leave a hitch-hiker by the side of the road.

I started considering the possibility of hiding the fridge and only revealing its existence when the driver had already stopped and committed to the lift. I concluded that this wasn't cheating but should be a measure resorted to only after about two hours or if it started to rain heavily. Neither proposition seemed too distant a prospect. I stood up. I tried smiling at cars. This didn't work and probably made me look certifiable. To ease the boredom, I tried to look nonplussed, just to see if it was possible. That must be a mark of a great actor – someone who can look nonplussed at the drop of a hat.

Just when I least expected it, in fact when I was having a go at looking bewildered, a scruffy red Fiesta van pulled over just in front of me. I couldn't believe it was stopping for me and ran forward to check. A dishevelled-looking old man and his Jack Russell surveyed me through the open window.

'I'm only going as far as Carrerreraragh,' he mumbled. Not the dog, the man.

At least that was what I thought he'd said; his accent was strong and he obviously felt that talking was best done with the mouth barely open.

'How far is Carr ... err ... eraragh?'

'You mean Carrecloughnarreraragh?'

'Yes, Car–, yes, there, how far is that?'

'Carrereraoughnarrara? It's about three miles.'

Oh God. Three miles is no use to anyone. From my previous experience of hitch-hiking I knew that it was sometimes better to turn down a lift than accept one that could land you in the middle of nowhere. I didn't like the sound of Carrerrererreragh, or its ability to sound different every time it was said. I tried to ascertain if Carreranoughnara would be any good for hitching.

'Is there anywhere round there I might–'

'Throw them in, throw them in.' He was pointing to my luggage.

'What's the road like there in Carra–'

'Throw them in, throw them in.' It might as well have been the dog talking for all the progress being made.

'I'm sorry, it's just that sometimes it's best to–'

'Look, jes' throw the feckin' things in the feckin' back, will ya?'

This did the trick. I responded immediately and against all my better judgement I was loading my gear into his tatty van in order to advance a further three miles up the road. Still, as I'd heard somewhere before, a journey of a thousand miles starts with one step.

Both he and the dog watched with interest as I lifted the fridge into the back.

'What have you got there?'

'It's a fridge.'

'Oh. You wouldn't want to be travellin' with a fridge for too long.'

Wouldn't you? No, I suppose you wouldn't. I got into the front seat and the dog jumped on to my lap, using me as a means of improving its view out of the front window.

'Where are you headed?' I asked.

'The cattle auction up the road here.'

'Are you going to buy a cow?'

'No, I'm just going to kill time.'

I suddenly felt a long way from home.

We arrived all too quickly in Carrerrerarse, the six minutes spent in the company of this mud-covered man and his dog having afforded me a brief respite from the notion that I had made a foolish error in my life. This hitching with a fridge business *was* possible. The man had stopped and he had picked up both me and my fridge. It was just bad luck that he was only going a few miles. And it was just bad luck that Carrerrerranoughnabollocks was one of the worst places for hitching in the Northern Hemisphere.

As the old man pulled into the side of the road, he was greeted by three other elderly farmer types who were also covered in mud. They weren't as muddy as him, obviously, but certainly muddy enough to be on the committee of the muddy gang. I got out, collected my gear and said goodbye, conscious of the fact that I was outside a cattle auction in the heart of rural Ireland, with a rucksack, a fridge and an insufficient coating of mud to be welcome in these parts.

All around me were the scenes of traffic congestion I had been dreaming of only minutes earlier. Trucks, wagons, carts, Range Rovers and tatty red Fiesta vans were arriving for the cattle auction and they were of absolutely no help to me. In fact, they were an enormous hindrance, making it something of a problem finding a place to stand where through traffic might see me. I lifted the fridge on to its trolley, hoisted the rucksack on to my back and started to walk up the road. Needless to say it was muddy. I looked round to wave goodbye, but the old man had gone and instead I saw his Jack Russell eyeing me disparagingly through the van's windscreen. Instinctively it seemed to know that the way I had chosen to travel lacked wisdom. I gave it the finger and continued.

As I walked I could hear the monotone machine-gunfire delivery of the cattle auctioneer over the distant PA. I hoped for his sake that his entire audience wasn't made up of those who were killing time. I walked on. A farmer was staring at me. What's his problem? I thought. I had forgotten that he had just seen an unmuddy man pulling a fridge behind him give the finger to a Jack Russell dog.

Presently I arrived at the hitching location that I considered the least unsuitable of those available to me. I was still alongside parked cars but I felt it was worth a try. Just as I had finished arranging myself as attractively as I could, it started to rain. Hard.

I had two alternatives. I could either commence an undignified struggle with my rucksack in an attempt to extricate my waterproofs, or I could go and seek shelter. The problem with the second option was that the only shelter available was the building in which the cattle auction was taking place, and I was frightened that a combination of despondency and delirium would see me making a successful bid for a cow. Hitching round Ireland with a fridge *and* a cow really would be pushing it.

With considerable trepidation I took on the rucksack. I had just opened it up and was subjecting the clothes at its apex to the full consequences of the weather conditions when, thank God, a car stopped for me. A blue Datsun estate car, a Sunny, or a Cherry, or one of those – no, I know what it was: the Datsun Saviour. I scurried to the passenger door and opened it.

'How far are you going?' I said.

The driver looked at me with consternation. 'I'm just parking here,' he replied.

This fridge hitch-hiking business was turning out to be harder than I thought it was going to be. I wonder why I had thought otherwise. Perhaps I'd considered, either consciously or subconsciously, that my status of being moderately well known for my TV work as a comedian might, as it had done in the past, open some doors to me that might otherwise have slammed shut in my face. But even if my modest fame in the UK had stretched as far as Ireland, the problem remained that, as a hitch-hiker, I was just a dot in the distance to the oncoming vehicle. By the time the car drew close by, the decision had already been made by the driver as to whether to stop.

So, as I stood there by the side of the road with my thumb out, waiting for the second lift of my heroic journey, it occurred to me that hitching is a great leveller. No hitcher is more special than another. When our beseeching thumbs are out, we all seem somehow equal.

We live in a world that constantly tells us that one person is better than another. Mark is better than Jeremy at football. Sue is better than Elise at music. Andy is better than Paul at schoolwork. George is better at starting wars than Tony.* It seems we've created a very competitive world for ourselves – perhaps needlessly.

As I stood by the side of the road with my thumb out, I realised there was nothing I could do that would make me *better than* any other hitch-hiker that came along. So no need to try. Just relax. How very liberating. My fridge journey had reminded me of something I instinctively knew, but that the busy world had drummed out of my consciousness. *I wasn't better than anyone else.*

Now hang on a minute – this wasn't something that the competitive world of showbusiness had taught me. Surely I was a better comedian than one who couldn't get as many laughs as me, or one who hadn't been on television as much as I had? Wasn't I better if I was richer or more famous?

This humbling roadside experience seemed to be teaching me exactly the opposite. I'm not *better than* anyone else, and no one is *better than* me. *Different from*, maybe, but not *better than*.

---

* Actually, when you think about it, perhaps they're each as good as the other.

In this moment of fridge-hiking failure, I was being taught that whatever material possessions, status, talents, skills or intelligence I may have had, it wasn't going to make a scrap of difference in how quickly and easily I progressed on this journey. It was a pretty level playing field all of a sudden. For the moment at least, I couldn't *buy* help. Neither could I trick, bargain, cajole or even fight for it. I just had to stand there by the side of the road and trust that help would come along, sooner or later.

In a way I had been stripped bare. Metaphorically naked though I may have been, standing in the driving rain getting slowly soaked, I became aware of something quite fundamental:

We are all equal in spirit.

HELP!

I remained by the roadside, beginning to believe that this fridge-hitching business was going to turn out to be the biggest mistake of my life.

A car ahead tooted its horn. It was obviously having some difficulty parking. The rain, which had temporarily stopped, began again and forlornly I went back to rummaging for waterproofs. Then the car ahead did something very strange. It went into reverse and stopped alongside me. The driver leant over, wound down the passenger window and said, 'I heard you on the radio this morning. I thought you'd be gone by now.'

I should explain something here that perhaps I should have told you earlier. When I first arrived in Ireland I met some people in a bar who, upon learning of my travel plans, made the following suggestion:

'You should phone Gerry Ryan,' they said. 'He loves wacky ideas. He'll love what you're doing.'

I followed their advice and found that getting through to the show was a surprisingly quick and easy process. After a preliminary brief chat with a producer, I was soon on air and discussing my adventure with the man himself, Gerry Ryan.

Interestingly, Gerry seemed instantly to understand

the concept of what I was doing – even though I still had no real idea myself.

'Tony, it sounds like a completely purposeless idea but a damn fine one,' he said during that first interview. 'Do call us from time to time and let us know how you're getting on.'

'I will, Gerry, thanks.'

What I didn't know, when I hung up after that first chat, was just how many people listened to this show, and how influential it could be in the country. The man in the car that had now stopped for me was going to make it very clear.

'I heard you talking on *The Gerry Ryan Show* this morning,' he said excitedly. 'I love what you're doing – fair play to yer – and I've been looking out for you all morning!'

I was in the company of Brendan, an enthusiastic travelling toiletries salesman who ended up taking me all the way to Donegal Town, the journey incorporating numerous stops at convenience stores along the way. We got on so well that when we reached Donegal Town, where Brendan was overnighting in a hotel and where I checked into a B&B, we decided to go for a few beers together.

Brendan and I drank in three pubs, the last being far and away my favourite. From the exterior there had been very little to suggest it was a pub: net curtains, an old lamp and a faded sign with a surname on it. In much of Ireland they don't go in for grand pub names like 'The Coach and Horses' or 'The Prince of Wales', they simply name it after the proprietor – 'Daly's' or 'McCarthy's', the first indication of the more personal experience that awaits you within. I came to call these establishments the old boys' pubs, where everybody talks to everybody else regardless of who they are, partly because the clientele are very friendly and partly because the clientele are very pissed.

Just like an orchestra will have a Lead Violinist, most pubs will have a Lead Drunk. Or Drunk in Residence. He must have some arrangement with the landlord that means he doesn't have to pay for any drinks which he can't say. His main role seems to be to welcome newcomers with the emission of a loud wailing noise and by flailing his arms about like a drowning man, until his already precarious hold on his own centre of gravity is upset to the point of liberating him totally from his bar stool. This is where the Second Drunk instinctively reaches out with his left hand to stop him falling to the ground and continues drinking with his right, as if the whole manoeuvre has been carefully rehearsed. Which of course it has. Every night for decades.

It wasn't long before Brendan and I were embroiled in a conversation with the regulars, the theme of which was prompted by highlights of today's Grand Prix on the TV screen behind the bar. I took a back seat in the discussion, largely due to an ignorance of motor racing and an inability to understand anything that was being said. As far as I could make out, the main thrust of it was the establishment of who came first, second and third.

The Lead Drunk was now almost comatose, the exertions of his initial greeting for us having taken their toll. Many names were put forward and rejected but after ten minutes of animated debate, the fact that Schumacher had won and Eddie Irvine had come third was settled upon and those present seemed content with what had been achieved. Suddenly, and out of nowhere, the Lead Drunk blurted out, 'Who came fifth?'

Everyone turned to him in shock. Where had this come from? This, from a man who had been folded up on top of his bar stool for the past quarter of an hour. Three questions troubled all of us. How had he followed what was going on, how had he managed his first intelligible sentence of the evening, and why did he care who came fifth?

'Who came fifth?' He repeated his extraordinary question but this time he felt it would be better bellowed. For the first time that night (and I suspect for a number of years), the bar's customers were completely silent. No one knew what crossing of wires in the drunk's brain had caused this enquiry, when 'Who came second?' had been the more relevant and 'Help!' the most suitable. More importantly, there was silence because no one actually knew who came fifth. When discussions finally got under way to solve this mystery, Brendan and I decided it was a signal to turn in for the night. Our 'one for the road' had turned into 'three for the road' and there was a danger of granting the road too much respect.

For now, I could congratulate myself on a great first day and celebrate the fact that if people had stopped for me and my fridge today, then why wouldn't they stop tomorrow? I was filled with positive thoughts. Help, I somehow knew, was on its way. Why did I feel so confident? How could I have been so sure that help was just around the corner?

Every time I set my fridge down by the side of the road and began hitch-hiking, my intention was clear. I was going to stand there and wait until a car stopped for me. Of one thing I was certain. *I wasn't going anywhere unless someone stopped for me.* If I didn't *believe* that someone would stop for me, then there would have been no point whatsoever in standing by the side of the road in the first place. All that sustains the hitch-hiker by the side of the road hitching is the *faith* that someone will stop and help you. And guess what? They always do. It might be a long old wait, but to my knowledge no one has starved to death by the side of the road waiting for someone to stop and give them a lift. It may be much harder in some locations and some cultures than others, but someone will always stop and help you in the end.

The media like to hype up what an awful place the world is, but a hitch-hiker will tell you otherwise.

I'm not going anywhere unless someone stops for me, but there are a lot of people out there waiting to help me. The extent to which I am able to enjoy my day is entirely dependent on how much faith I have in the second of these two facts.

If you need people to help you, and most of us do at some point or another, the good news is that these people are already out there, driving along the road, ready to offer a helping hand. All you need to do is put yourself out there, in the right positive spirit, so that you are ready to receive their assistance. Then just wait patiently for your helpers to come along.

That's exactly what I was doing on my fridge adventure. Without help the journey was a non-starter. I didn't know when the help was coming, but I knew it was out there. Life became so much simpler once I recognized this. After all, when you peel away all the paraphernalia and complications of life, there are only really two things we need to do every day of our lives.

Help others.

Allow others to help us.

So often we are taught to be fearful and untrusting.

For the most part we are alerted to the dangers that people may bring us rather than the aid they may offer.

'Be careful.'

Wasn't that what we were always being taught? Is it any wonder that this is how we live our lives? Being careful – on the lookout for that bad thing that's just waiting to happen. I'll admit that there is a balance to be struck and that we need to be responsible and use our common sense, but perhaps instead of always being 'careful', we could learn to find the moments when it serves us to be 'carefree'.

It can open a lot more doors and end up being a lot more fun.

We're often taught by our peers, our parents and the media that people are out to get you. In fact, most of them aren't. Most of them will help you nine times out of ten. People like helping people. It makes them feel good. It actually makes people happy. When was the last time you helped someone? Perhaps you gave assistance to an elderly person or helped someone who was struggling with some bags. How did you feel when the other person thanked you? Of course, you felt good. You felt good about yourself and you felt good about what you'd done.

What would our lives be like if we recognised that other people *want* to help us? How would our days unfold if we trained ourselves to look at people and *expect* them to be kind to us and offer assistance? There is a lot of power in that expectation. A hitch-hiker knows this, even if he is encumbered with a fridge.

There are a lot of people out there
waiting to help you.

A STRETCH OF ROAD

I began my second day by calling RTE radio and giving Gerry Ryan an update on how things were going. He was most impressed by my progress and declared on air that Donegal Town by the end of Day One was 'absolutely bloody marvellous'. I explained that I was heading for Bunbeg, where I hoped to get a ferry out to Tory Island, thus fulfilling one of the terms of the bet. At the end of our interview, I was told that someone had called in while we were on air and offered me free accommodation in Bunbeg, and I took down the details, staggered that my quest was being greeted with such a positive response.

Moments after I'd arranged myself by the roadside and almost before I was mentally prepared for my next lift, a huge truck slammed on its brakes and came to a standstill forty yards ahead. Leaving my stuff, I ran ahead to see if it was stopping for me or to avoid running something over. The truck was so big, I could only just reach the handle of the cabin door. I opened it and the driver said, 'Are you Tony?'

'Yes.'

'Well, go and get your fridge.'

It was a long way up into that truck, and the cabin was surprisingly small, its crampedness compounded by a fridge wedged behind my seat. The lack of space seemed a little ironic given that we were pulling a forty-five-foot trailer behind us.

After formal introductions (well, as formal as they could be in this situation), I learned that I was in the company of Jason, a man in his early twenties beaming with excitement and who wasted no time in peppering me with questions.

'What are you doing with that fridge anyways?'

'Well, I'm travelling with it to win a bet with someone.'

'You're mad. I was listening to you on the radio this morning and I was in stretches.'

I wasn't sure what stretches were, but Jason was smiling so I assumed they were good.

'I've been keeping an eye out for you.'

'Brilliant. That's very kind of you.'

'I didn't know who you were until I saw that fridge, and then I thought ...'

Laughter took him over for a while, before he managed, 'Ah, it's all a good laugh.'

Good, he understands.

I took a moment to digest it all. Hang on. Something else was happening here. He thought the fridge was a *good* thing. In fact, it had been because of the fridge that he'd stopped for me. The fridge, far from being a hindrance, had become a positive thing, and the protagonist in an excursion that was growing ever more surreal.

From the haven of the truck's cabin I watched the driving rain pelt against the windscreen and felt somehow invincible, especially when Jason announced that he was going to my chosen destination – Bunbeg. All right, I'd have to wait while he did some deliveries but I didn't mind that. Why should I? Yesterday I'd done toiletry sales – today groceries, deliveries thereof. And I was seeing first hand what makes the world tick – good honest labour.

A few hours later, after Jason had let me off in what he called Bunbeg and what most of us would call a stretch of road, it had stopped raining completely. Around me there was a hotel, a couple of houses, a lot of open space and a lovely view of a sandy bay. My free accommodation had been offered at Bunbeg House, which the radio people had told me was down by the harbour. Enquiries in the hotel produced directions and my first piece of bad news. In polite conversation I had allowed it to become known that I was headed for Tory Island. This was greeted with a shake of the head and, 'But you won't be able to get out there until Friday.' It turned out that once a year the ferry was taken down to Killybegs for a complete refurbishment, and it had gone for this year's earlier that morning.

This meant the ferry was out of action for three days. Oh dear. Oh dear, oh dear. A setback of substantial proportions. Getting to Tory Island was a condition of the bet and, just at this moment, spending three days in a stretch of road seemed a bit too long.

However, I was about to meet Andy, the cockney proprietor of the guesthouse that had offered me free accommodation, and he was an optimist by nature.

'We'll get you out to Tory Island, don't worry,' he said, before marching me up the road to lead me to the local pub.

Once inside, the clientele were informed of my predicament with regard to getting out to Tory Island. The whole pub then seemed to mobilise in search of a solution.

I soon had the phone numbers of five fishermen who might be going out to Tory Island in the morning, and coins were thrust into my hand as I was dispatched to the payphone to follow up these leads. But alas, nothing. I kept hearing a polite and regretful 'No, I can't help you.' The fishing must have been poor out that way because no one, but no one, was going there.

'Why doesn't he try Patsy Dan?' someone said.

'Who's Patsy Dan?' I asked.

'He's the King of Tory.'

'What?'

'Patsy Dan Rogers – he's the King of Tory.'

I had heard right. Tory Island has a long tradition of having its own monarch, and the present incumbent was Patsy Dan.

I was given his phone number. This was unusual in itself. I imagine that most of the time the personal phone numbers of kings aren't handed out in pubs as a matter of course.

'Well, what use is ringing him?' I enquired.

'He might be able to organise something from his end.'

And so I found myself once again making my way to a pub payphone urged on by a pubload of locals, this time to phone a king and explain that I needed to get myself and a fridge out to his island as a matter of some urgency. It was Tuesday night. I had set off on Monday morning. I couldn't have expected things to develop thus far in such a short period of time.

'Hello, is that Patsy Dan?' I said, with a small group of my more fervent followers standing near the telephone in support.

'It is.' He had a deep, gravelly voice.

'Are you the King of Tory?'

'That I am, yes.'

'Good. I was wondering if you could help. I'm travelling round Ireland with a fridge to win a bet and I need to get out to Tory Island to complete the first part of that bet, but as you probably know, the ferry isn't running …' and so I went on. Patsy listened intently and seemed to find nothing unusual in my quest.

'Of course we would love you to come to Tory, and I shall be happy to greet you on your arrival, so I shall give you the following numbers you can ring to find if anyone is coming out to the island.'

He spoke at great length in a very deliberate manner and proceeded to give me the names and numbers of all the fishermen I had already telephoned. I resisted the temptation of saying 'Thanks for nothing,' or asking him why the royal yacht hadn't been made available.

Moments later a girl came through from the public bar and told us that she had been talking with a load of guys from the Air Corps, who were stationed nearby. A voice piped up, 'Bejaysus, that's it! We'll get yer man out by helicopter!'

There was a split second of silence followed by overwhelming approval. That was it: the mob had their hearts on my reaching Tory Island by helicopter. There wasn't one dissenter.

'Come on, Tone, let's go and 'ave a word wiv 'em,' said Andy, his accent a reminder of home, and a more rational world I had left behind. And off we went to the public bar where I was encouraged to stand before a group of servicemen and make my 'pitch' for a helicopter. I wasn't sure about this at all. I made a poor start, which deteriorated rapidly when I attempted to casually throw in the involvement of a fridge in all this, and I could see the expressions of the servicemen change from curious to baffled. I lost my way and Andy took over. 'Now, boys, we're not being silly 'ere, this man has got to get out to Tory Island, he's got national coverage on the radio and if we can get him out there, it'll be good for tourism – both for Tory Island and for us round here. Now I know it's not for you to worry about and that you're not from round here yerselves, but think of the good press you'd get if you 'elp out on this one and all the good feeling you'll get in the community.'

He was doing well. He went on, 'Now come on, one of you boys must be prepared to take your chopper out for him.'

All that good work undone in one careless turn of phrase.

We emerged from the public bar, Andy's glib sales pitch having eventually fallen on sympathetic ears. The pilots said they were up for helping out and had given us the name of a woman from the Ministry of Defence in Dublin, whom we would have to ask to authorise such a 'mercy mission'. We returned to the main bar fairly confident that she would: 'She will, won't she?' 'Course she will.' A common enough conversation between two men in a bar but usually with reference to less noble matters.

We allowed drink to inflate a moderate success into a magnificent triumph. It was taken as read by all and sundry that in the morning I would be flying to Tory Island by helicopter. Any doubts I might have still had were soon vanquished by the constant flow of pints, which continued into the night.

'You see what you can do when you put your mind to it,' said Andy.

I could. When you put your mind to it, you could get very pissed.

It was time to say goodnight.

'Gernye.'

'Gonnye. Caw blesya.'

We knew what we meant.

I suppose I should have gone to bed feeling down in the dumps. The ferry not being available had been something that was preventing me from achieving what I'd set out to do. Okay, there was the possibility of the helicopter supplied by the Ministry of Defence in Dublin, but a sober man would have known this was almost certainly a pipedream.

So here I was – unable to get out to Tory Island, and yet not remotely fed up. Well, with all the help, kindness and hospitality I was receiving, how could I be? Maybe I wasn't getting out to Tory Island, but something else was certainly happening. And the 'something else' that was happening was warm, uplifting and, above all, great fun.

It wasn't until months later when I was seated at a desk attempting to write a book about the adventures I'd had on my fridge journey that I fully came to appreciate just how advantageous this setback really was. Why? Well, I knew that if the protagonist had to overcome a few hurdles along the way and it wasn't all too easy, then my story would make for a far more interesting read. As a writer, I was very grateful that something on my journey had 'gone wrong'.

Once again the 'bad' thing had become a 'good' thing.

Wow! How amazing, I thought, if you could live your life like that. Bad things become good things. Incredible. I realised there and then:

An obstacle is an opportunity.

The idea that an obstacle could be an opportunity is not something most of us recognise as we dash through our hectic days. We jump to conclusions and make hasty decisions about what is good and bad.

'It's bad that I've missed this train.'

'It's bad that I've lost my job.'

'It's bad that my boyfriend/girlfriend has left me.'

Well, how do we *know*? That girlfriend or boyfriend who broke our heart when we were in our teens – would we take them back now if they were on offer? Probably not. It felt like a bad thing at the time, but hindsight has shown us that this wasn't necessarily the case at all.

The whole fridge experience has helped me to look at things differently when they don't go to plan. It's taught me that if I change my view of the situation by thinking of it as an opportunity, it can dramatically change the nature of what is before me. Just by viewing things with a different slant you can find your energy levels are so much higher and you're more positive about everything. Sometimes, as a result, 'lucky things' may even start to happen.

Throughout my journey in Ireland I was on such a 'high' (largely as a result of the events that unfolded around me and my fridge) that I was able to receive any setback with a wry smile. And later I discovered that however irritating the problem may have seemed at the time, in the long term I would benefit from it – even if it just provided a humorous chapter in a book.

Time, it is often said, is a healer. A cliché perhaps, but one that is rooted in truth. Time gives us perspective. How often have we been able to look back at something that upset us terribly years ago and then make a joke about it today? We know now that it was a stepping stone on a path to becoming a stronger, more mature person.

It's just stuff that's happening. That's all. Go with it. Concentrate instead on the nice clear stretch of road that lies ahead, and the supposed 'bad stuff' will soon feel like a small town you've left far behind.

THE PARABLE OF THE
POOR KING

Our failure to find a boat to take me to Tory Island had produced the bonus of a free morning, which I intended to spend reading and relaxing.

I was being naively optimistic. The fridge journey was gaining an unexpected momentum. People knew where I was, and I was in demand. All morning the phone didn't stop ringing for me, and Andy's dining room turned into my office. I began by giving another interview to *The Gerry Ryan Show*, in which Gerry instructed 'all of Ireland' to put on their thinking caps and come up with some means to get me out to Tory Island. RTE television called almost as soon as I'd finished on the radio. An afternoon show called *Live at Three* had heard about me from Gerry's show and were keen to send a presenter and a mobile unit to film me hitching by the roadside. They wanted to know where I would be on Friday. So did I. I tried to explain this, but it was a difficult concept to grasp for someone in the Filofax 'Let's do lunch' world of television.

'But you must know where you're going to be. Do you not have a game plan?'

'My game plan is not to have a game plan,' I said, being deliberately nebulous.

Antoinette, to whom I was talking, was torn between being genuinely amused by the whole notion of 'fridge hitch-hiking', and being frustrated by the guaranteed uncertainties that appeared to be a part of it. She seemed to be the producer, researcher *and* presenter on *Live At Three*, and I half expected our conversation to be cut short at any minute because she had to go and do some make-up or operate Camera 4. She called three more times in the space of an hour with more questions to which I could offer no satisfactory answers. I wasn't making her life easy with my 'I don't knows', 'maybes' and 'probablys', and I could have been more helpful, but there was a certain power afforded to me as a result of my not really caring whether I did this programme or not, and I wasn't going to squander it.

'Look, Tony, you mad eejit, I'll ring you later – but this is how we'll leave it for now. My intention is to get someone to drive you to wherever the mobile unit are going to be on Friday and then drive you back to wherever you would have got to if you'd spent that day doing an ordinary day's hitch-hiking.'

This, apparently, made sense to her.

Sometimes the outbreak of war can release a heroic side to a person's nature. It was Andy's personal tragedy that his had been released by the arrival of a man and a fridge. For when the bad news was received that *The Gerry Ryan Show* had taken *no* calls with regard to the Tory Island appeal, Andy sprang to life, making phone call after phone call and declaring, 'Don't worry, Tone, we'll get you out there.'

The name of the person the Air Corps had given us the previous evening meant nothing to anyone in the Ministry of Defence, but Andy didn't give up. He called the Air Corps direct, rang local press, contacted the local TD (MP) for the area, and after forty-five minutes of almost continuous bullshit he eventually acquired the telephone number of the top nob in the Ministry of Defence in Dublin. We just needed him to give clearance for the Air Corps to fly me out. Andy's 'moment' had arrived. He had already demonstrated that he could talk persuasive nonsense but it had all been a rehearsal for this call.

He was fantastic. I listened in wonder as he managed to convince a Dublin bureaucrat that it was vitally important to get a man and a fridge airlifted out to a tiny, sparsely populated Atlantic island.

'... you see he's from England, and they're following the story over there and I've been inundated with phone calls this morning with press wanting to know how he's getting on. It's a big disaster for us up here because this is one of the biggest chances we've got to promote Donegal and Tory Island – and we're all in complete shock because the last thing we expected was this ferry to be broke down and we're all gutted because everyone put so much work into this ... this is a big bombshell, everyone was running round last night trying to 'elp ... yeah ... yeah ... I understand that ... right. It's just I don't want to be the one going back to the committee saying that we failed on this one. If we let Tone down, we let Ireland down and we lose out on millions of pounds of tourist revenue.'

I blushed a little. Andy hung up and turned to me.

'This is it – the end of the road. They've promised

that they're going to ring me back in twenty minutes and let me know one way or the other.'

'What do you think the chances are?'

'Good. Pretty good. He really did seem like he wanted to 'elp.'

I was getting quite excited. I'd never been in a helicopter before.

Hang on, though. Hadn't I read somewhere that the helicopter is the single most dangerous form of air transport? I became jittery; I tried to calm down by assuring myself that it was only the take-off and landing that were hazardous. Then I realised that given the short nature of this flight, taking off and landing was virtually *all* we were going to do.

I needn't have worried, however, because twenty minutes later the Ministry of Defence rang to say they were sorry but they couldn't help.

Oh dear.

We consoled ourselves with meaningless platitudes like 'Maybe it's for the best this way,' 'Well, at least we tried,' and unsurprisingly it did little to ease the pain. Andy looked most dejected. After all, he had spent hours on what many would have described as a pointless mission, and all his efforts had been futile. He left, presumably to renew his acquaintance with his wife and family, and to run some errands that should have already been run. I wandered down to the quayside to check out the possibilities of finding a fishing boat that might be making the journey the next day. If that failed, I might have to throw in the towel as far as Tory Island was concerned.

Outside, a few yards from Bunbeg House, I could see a rugged-looking fisherman on his hands and knees messing about with tackle. I coughed self-consciously to get his attention.

'Hello, I don't know whether you'll be able to help, I'm trying to get out to Tory Island, the ferry won't be running for a while, and I'm trying to find out if you know of any boats which might be going out there at all.'

He regarded me with some surprise.

'Rory McClafferty was away an hour ago.'

'What?'

'Rory McClafferty is just after leaving. Around an hour ago, I'd say. He left with a load of blocks he's taking out there.'

'You mean, he left in a boat, from this quayside, to go to Tory Island?' I couldn't believe what I was hearing.

'Ah yes, he was away about an hour ago. You say you wanted to get out to Tory?'

'You could say that.' I pointed to the dining room of Bunbeg House. 'We've been in there all morning organising appeals over the air on national radio and trying to get the Ministry of Defence to clear a helicopter to get me out to Tory Island.'

'Oh, you'll get nothing in there,' he said, pointing into the dining room. I had to admire the terse accuracy of this remark.

'Will anyone else be going out there today, do you think?'

'Not now, not with the tide the way it is.' He looked up from his nets and eyed me quizzically. 'Were you not down at the pier this morning?'

'Er … no.'

'Well, if you'd been down at the pier this morning, someone would have told you about Rory and you'd be on the island now.'

Of course I would. I had made a terrible mistake. I

had trusted in the local knowledge of Andy, a man who came from Bermondsey.

'He'll be going out again tomorrow morning though. He'll be able to take you then, if you still want to go.'

'I do. Tell him I most definitely do.'

'I will, so I will.'

While Andy had valiantly embarked on the fruitless endeavour of securing a helicopter, a friendly fishing boat had left for the desired destination from literally a matter of yards away. Telephoning fishermen the night before had proved to be no substitute for wandering down to the quayside and asking. As I walked the five or six yards back to Bunbeg House, I was struck by the lesson that was to be learned here. Be ambitious, strive for great heights and don't give up without a fight – but don't do so without first exploring the simple option. I decided to spare Andy the news until later, thinking it might spoil his day still further.

Back in Bunbeg House I received yet another call from Antoinette from *Live at Three*, and this time she was even more intolerant of my indecisiveness, making it clear that they had a slot in the programme in two days' time and asking if I could do it. Poor old Antoinette could do without a ditherer like me.

'Look, don't you commit to anything in your life?' she said, her words a chilling echo of accusations fired at me by at least two past girlfriends.

Thrown off balance by the resonance of this remark, I thoughtlessly agreed to do the show, not realising that by so doing I had put in jeopardy the romantic ideal of spending at least one night on an isolated island. The plans to which I had agreed involved a bloke called Gary picking me up at 10.30 the following morning and driving me to wherever the mobile unit was going to be. My trip to Tory would have to be a brief one, it seemed.

On the crossing the next day, Rory was interested to note that I was carrying a bouquet of flowers.

'Who are they for?' he enquired.

'They're for the King of Tory's daughter.'

He gave me a look that could have meant so many things, except of course, 'Good idea.'

The flowers were an act of silliness on my part – but when travelling with a fridge, silliness comes easy. I'd heard that the king had a daughter called Bridey, and, largely to amuse people in the pub, I'd said that it might be a good move to try and woo her, since marrying into royalty could only be a good thing.

The fishing boat docked at the tiny harbour in West Town. (The use of the word 'town' was generous given that the entire population of the island was not much more than a hundred. I learned later that the cluster of crofts on the other side of the island was known as East Town. The imaginative naming of their settlements didn't appear to be one of the islanders' strong points.)

Patsy Dan, the King of Tory, had agreed to meet me in his croft and I was quite excited as I'd never met a king before.

After a five-minute struggle pulling a fridge up narrow dirt tracks, I was standing outside the tiny cottage that doubled as a royal palace. I knocked on the door and seconds later there appeared a stocky, rugged-looking man with a fair moustache and a peaked cap where his crown ought to have been.

Patsy Dan greeted me with a 'Failte' (Gaelic for 'Welcome') and asked me about the flowers.

'They're for your daughter because she's a princess and princesses merit flowers.'

'Oh dear,' he replied. 'She's not on the island. She left this morning to go to the mainland for a couple of days.'

They say that timing is the secret of good comedy. It helps in courtship sometimes too.

I tested the king's sense of humour by explaining to him that I had hoped to marry his daughter and thus become a prince. He treated my comment in all seriousness.

'Oh my goodness, well, I don't know that it would be so easy but you would have to do a lot of talking and a number of meetings and so on. Would you like a cup of tea?'

Patsy Dan and I talked over tea in his humble abode, here in this remote outpost in the Atlantic. It was my first audience with a king and it was an undoubted success. We liked each other, and the king was filled with admiration for my fridge journey, mainly because he was convinced, despite my two attempts to persuade him otherwise, that I was not hitching but walking round Ireland with a fridge.

As if I'd do something as stupid as that.

Upon my departure, Patsy Dan shook my hand and uttered his most memorable words thus far:

'You know, Tony, I may be the poorest king on Earth but I am a happy one.'

This had a nice ring to it, and a fair measure of profundity. Of course, it might just have been a line that rolled off the tongue for tourists, and the truth might have been altogether different, but as the boat pulled out of the harbour and he stood on the pier smiling and waving, I liked to think that he understood, better than some, how to handle life, love and monarchy.

The king's words have refused to leave me. Patsy Dan seemed to be the living proof of the old cliché that money doesn't make you happy. I'd suspected as much in the past, but now there seemed to be some concrete evidence. By living simply, the King of Tory appeared to be faring considerably better than most of the royal families on the planet.

In terms of my material possessions, on this fridge journey at least, I was just like Patsy Dan. I had no wealth to offer anyone except my friendship. All I had was a rucksack containing the bare essentials and a fridge containing a washbag and some shoes. And yet I too was as happy. I was happy because each day was another joyful experience filled with laughter, friendship and downright silliness. What else did I need?

We don't exactly live in an environment where we are urged to make the best of what we've got. Ours is not a world where we are encouraged to buy *less* and want *less* – and it could be argued that this leaves a fair few of us feeling hope*less*. Most days we are bombarded with a stream of advertisements imploring us to buy a better car, lawnmower, TV, computer or mobile phone. On top of that, newspaper articles and TV programmes suggest that we improve our looks, our clothes, our homes and our general lifestyles. All the time we are brainwashed into expecting more and more. This leads to disappointment or unhappiness when the 'more' ends up being beyond our means, or something doesn't deliver what we thought it was going to.

Hitch-hiking spared me this daily dose of poison. Most of the time I was by the roadside or in people's cars – or in pubs or small bed and breakfasts. Apart from my conversations with *The Gerry Ryan Show*, I was beyond the reach of the media and all its materialistic influences.

My life had become very simple. All I needed to do was get up, put my fridge by the side of the road and head in a certain direction. It was pointless trying to acquire more stuff. Why did I need more than I already had? More possessions would only make my load heavier and slow me down. This made me think. What would I be like when this journey was over and I got back to London? What would I be like when work, television, advertising hoardings and newspapers got their claws back into me? Would I desire more possessions again? If so, how could I be sure that what I'd be striving to acquire wouldn't make my load heavier and end up slowing me down?

I have always been impressed by the Native American Winnebago tribe, who had the tradition of burying their dead along with their possessions. As a consequence of this, it was customary for them to give most of their possessions away when they were still alive. They presumed that the recipients of their gifts would return the favour by looking after them later in life. Well, why wouldn't they?

Sometimes I wonder whether the structure of our society forces most people to live life slightly upside down. We work as hard as we can when we're young and fit (very often forgetting that work should be enjoyable), so that we can retire and have a lot of time off. Then, instead of benefiting from the fruits of our hard-earned labour, often we continue to live relatively frugally so that we can make out a generous will, thus only making our generosity count when we're dead.

Wouldn't it be better to give now? What are we waiting for? And this 'giving' doesn't have to mean giving in material terms – it can mean giving in the way we live our lives. We can give with a smile, a gesture, a comforting word or by forgiving, by encouraging and by praising.

Maybe we should turn our attention to giving a little bit *today*. After all, if you have a roof over your head, and enough food to survive, aren't people the most important parts of your life? Look around you. Do we really need even more?

We need less than we think we do.

'TOO LAID BACK FOR YOUR OWN GOOD'

Nine miles of water known as Tory Sound separates Tory Island from the shore. Some of this water is notoriously treacherous, being exposed to strong winds and dangerous currents. In the winter the island can be isolated from the mainland for up to a month at a time, and it's quite common for boats to be unable to make the crossing for three consecutive days. On the return journey Rory McClafferty told me, rather cruelly I think, about the centuries-old tradition of fishermen in these parts not learning to swim. Further to that, many hundreds of years ago the fishing communities in these areas had settled on the quaint custom of *not saving anyone who fell into the water*. This wasn't based on an ungenerous '*You* fell in, *you* get yourself out' policy, but on the superstitious belief that any encounter with the sea was preordained, and any act of rescue (including any attempt to swim yourself out of trouble) was an obstruction of fate's natural course, which would only bring tragedy upon yourself and your family. So, if some unlucky fisherman slipped overboard, instead of rushing to his aid, colleagues would run to the side of the boat shouting, 'Chuck us your watch,' or 'Can I have your dining table?' Needless to say, on the distinctly choppy crossing, I didn't do too much hanging over the side to take impressive photographs.

Of course, I didn't have to leave Tory Island when I did.

'Will you stay the night on Tory?' Patsy Dan had asked.

Tory island was a fascinating place. A remote Atlantic outpost, three miles long and half a mile wide, home to a hundred or so inhabitants divided up between the ever so slightly overstated East Town and West Town. The island had been inhabited since prehistoric times and was desolate, rocky and barren. Its current population lived off the fishing, with a few having sidelines as artists, painting landscapes with a naivety that had won them acclaim. Staying on the island longer would undoubtedly have been an interesting experience.

I'd been faced with a difficult choice. I'd been told there was a storm coming in and that the possibility of being stuck on the island for a few days was a real one. Antoinette at *Live at Three* wouldn't have appreciated that too much.

'I'd love to stay over,' had been my reply to Patsy Dan, 'but I think I'd better leave while I can.'

I made the choice.

Every day we are faced with lots of choices. In fact, if you think about it, our days are made up with little else. Shall I get up now? Shall I have a cup of coffee? Shall I listen to the radio? Shall I drive to work? Shall I overtake that car? Where shall I sit on the train?

Shall I continue to read this slightly tedious list of questions? (It has ended now anyway so you don't have a choice.*)

My dilemma wasn't a complicated one. Shall I stay on the island – or shall I leave with Rory McClafferty and be sure of keeping my commitment to Antoinette and RTE television?

I made the choice. And then, once I'd made it, and Rory had cast the ropes ashore and started to guide his fishing boat out of Tory's tiny harbour, I didn't think to bother myself about whether it had been the right decision. What was done was done. No point in looking back. I kept my eyes keenly focused on the road ahead, which, on this particular occasion, happened to be an irritatingly choppy bit of sea.

The journey with Gary, Antoinette's friend and temporary driver for RTE, was a fraught one. Maps were lost and many a wrong turn was taken. The RTE mobile TV unit was awaiting us just outside Crossmaglen in Northern Ireland, which Gary described as 'Republican bandit country'. Arriving only five minutes before the show went on air caused Antoinette a few heart palpitations.

'Jeez, where the hell have you been?' she gasped. 'We were just working out how to fill seven minutes of airtime.'

---

* Other than to put the book down and go and play football, do some cooking, visit friends, write your diary, go shopping, pay some utility bills, complain to the council about something that needs complaining about, or start compiling a list of all the things you could do if you weren't reading this.

She looked me up and down.

'You must be Tony, the nutter with the fridge. I'll have to get to know you on air because we're on in five.'

Why Antoinette's producer had chosen this location for a roadside interview was a mystery. Quite apart from it being in another country to the one I was hitching in, it was probably the noisiest stretch of road for miles around. No doubt the producer had his reasons, and no doubt they were crap.

I chatted well enough, though, my conversations with Gerry Ryan having left me adept in the patter required to explain all that I was about, and the interview went very smoothly. I stood by the roadside with my fridge, and Antoinette fired questions at me while I hitched. It couldn't have gone much better. Okay, the occasional juggernaut hurtled past drowning out everything that was being said, but this didn't seem to bother the producer, who was more than happy.

At the end of the interview Antoinette presented me with three indelible marker pens, with which I was to get those who had given me lifts to sign my fridge. What a good idea. Then, as I had been asked to do, I announced that I was going to look for a better spot to hitch, and pulled my fridge up the road and away from the cameras, allowing Antoinette to do her final piece to camera. When we went off air, I stopped and looked up at a road sign that was now above me. It had a picture of a man in a balaclava, and below it were written the words:

SNIPER AT WORK

Thank you, RTE. They had brought me to one of the most dangerous locations in all of Ireland and had encouraged me to swan around with a fridge.

I was driven, as agreed, back to Sligo, where I could continue my hitching, and Antoinette turned out to be my designated driver for this portion of the journey. In her slightly bashed-up car we made the journey to Sligo through Monaghan, Fermanagh and County Leitrim. It was a pretty drive and the latter stages prompted a drawing of breath, with Glencar Lake on one side and the imposing Dartry mountains rising above us on the other. We were in Yeats country, so called because Sligo was where WB and his famous family once resided. They were quite a talented lot, the Yeatses; his brother Jack and father John were both considered to be fine artists. WB Yeats himself always professed to have a deep affection for the countryside of his childhood and wrote, 'In a sense, Sligo has always been my home.' In what sense, though? In the sense that he chose to live almost anywhere else? Honestly, the stuff poets get away with, just because they've got a good turn of phrase. All right, he chose to be buried in Sligo, but it has always struck me as more of a compliment to a place to spend time there when you're alive, rather than dead. Like Yeats, I too would happily choose to see out my days on the French Riviera, but where me and WB differ is that I don't care where you bury me.

Antoinette was worried about where I was going to stay.

'Have you booked anywhere?'

'Nope.'

'Have you got a brochure with details of accommodation?'

'Nope. The right place will come along.'

'Tony, you're too laid back for your own good.'

'I'm not that laid back, I just have faith.'

'In what?'

A pause. I didn't know exactly.

My laissez-faire attitude was simply the result of another choice. This time it was a simple one – not to be concerned about what was coming. The fridge journey had already taught me that I didn't need to be sure of details (like what, exactly, I had faith in). I just needed to have the confidence that everything would be okay, enabling me to make simple choices.

We forget that we have a choice about everything. Sometimes we'll tell ourselves that we don't, but when we do that we're deluding ourselves. We *do* have a choice – it's just that we don't necessarily like the consequences of that choice. Some are tough – very tough. Gandhi, in his dealings with the British Raj in India, chose not to cooperate with some of the laws that were introduced and as a result he went to prison on many occasions. He demonstrated that we always have a choice, even if the consequences may be unpalatable.*

On my fridge journey I had the usual set of choices like: what time shall I get up? What shall I have for breakfast? Others weren't so straightforward: shall I call *The Gerry Ryan Show*? Shall I do the interview on *Live at Three*? Shall I drink this fifth pint of Guinness that has been bought for me?

Yes, the choices were constant – they always are – but fundamentally I only really ever made one important decision each day:

What side of the road shall I stand on?

*Gandhi always saw prison as an opportunity to highlight injustice and gain publicity and momentum for his cause, and was therefore a master at turning an obstacle into an opportunity.

That was it. That was the extent of my responsibility on this adventure. Everything else I could leave to unfold. It is only now, many years after the event, that I can see that this was what contributed to the magic of the journey and the buoyant mood that sustained me throughout. Unwittingly, I had shed myself of worry. I was just living every day as it came and making the most of it.

Life was easier and more enjoyable – and I had so much more to offer to the world – because I had freed myself. Every day I only had to make one important choice. You can do the same.

Decide in what direction you want to travel.

How do I know what my direction is supposed to be? Well, put that thought on hold because we're going to come to that in the very next chapter. For now, just try to embrace the simple concept of life being a journey that requires a general direction.

Even though my fridge journey may have been relaxed, stress-free and devoid of any planning, there was still a general direction of travel. Dublin was where I was ultimately headed, and if the bet was going to be won, then that was where me and the fridge needed to get ourselves.

Our lack of any burdens might have made us seem weightless – but we were certainly not aimless. We knew exactly where we needed to go. Luckily, we were about to meet a very special person who would show us how to get there.

DUCK EGGS

When Antoinette and I reached Sligo (the largest town in Ireland's north-west), we parked in the main street and had a mosey around. I couldn't see anywhere I fancied staying and I wasn't sure whether I wanted to spend a Friday night in a town centre. Antoinette led me into a delicatessen hoping to buy a type of seaweed called 'dilisc', but unfortunately they had sold out. Never mind, the old man in the shop had a pleasing way about him that I instantly liked, and there was a huge egg on the counter which caught my attention.

'What's that?' I asked him.

'It's a duck egg.'

'How much is it?'

'What do you want a duck egg for?'

'I don't know, I just like the look of it. How much is it?'

'Don't be so silly, you don't want a duck egg.'

'I do. I want to buy this duck egg off you.'

'No, now come on, what would you want with a duck egg?'

Whatever happened to the aggressive hard sell? I couldn't buy this bloody duck egg off him until I could prove that I really needed it. And I couldn't, so the duck

egg remained in the delicatessen until a more suitable home was found for it.

The one hotel I enquired at was full, but I didn't like the look of it much anyway. However, we needed refreshing after the drive, so Antoinette and I had a quick drink in its dingy bar, where I noticed a sign that read:

STRICTLY NO SINGING

I had never seen a sign like this before, and it struck me as rather harsh. I mean, you may as well go the whole hog and have a sign up saying:

STRICTLY NO HAVING A GOOD TIME

It hadn't escaped Antoinette's notice that thus far here in Sligo I had failed to fall on my feet.

'So, this "faith" of yours hasn't exactly come up trumps with accommodation.'

'Not yet, no.'

'Perhaps it would help if you knew what it was you had faith in?'

'Oh, one doesn't want to worry oneself with unnecessary details.'

Antoinette was still a sceptic, but there was time to convert her.

'You know, I think I *do* know what I have faith in. I have faith in the fridge.'

I sounded like a man who was becoming delirious. Maybe I was. Perhaps the excesses and surreal events of the last few days had taken their toll.

'You too can have faith in the fridge,' I continued, each word edging me closer to committal. I wasn't an impressive proselytiser, and you needed to be when you were asking someone to have faith in a fridge. During the car journey I had expounded the credo that wherever you go, good things will happen to you, provided that you truly believe they will.

As we sat in this third-rate establishment where not even a natural expression of human joy like singing was permitted, it appeared the validity of my philosophy was in question. Then it came to me.

'We'll ask the man in the delicatessen where I could stay.'

'What?'

'Come on, finish your drink, let's go and ask the man in the delicatessen.'

I was testing this poor girl's levels of tolerance to the very limit, but her protestations weren't vociferous enough to prevent a return to the delicatessen and a question for the elderly proprietor.

'If you could stay anywhere in the Sligo area, where would you stay?'

He wasn't remotely taken aback. I had thought he would be expecting me to have another crack at purchasing the duck egg.

'Expensive or not expensive?'

'Doesn't matter.'

'Have you got a car?'

'Yes.'

I rather boldly assumed that Antoinette wasn't going to tire of my indulgent behaviour and dump me and my fridge on the streets of Sligo.

'Well, Strandhill is very nice.'

'Is that where you would go and stay, given the choice?'

He thought for a moment.

'Yes, I think it is. You could try the Ocean View Hotel, or there are a couple of bed and breakfasts down on the front.'

And very nice they were too, overlooking a broad expanse of sandy beach complete with panorama of evening sun setting over the Atlantic Ocean. I resolved that this was the place for me, the presence of a nice-looking pub within spitting distance having no bearing on my decision. Both B&Bs had vacancies, but I plumped for the one that had bathrooms en suite, deciding that it was worth the two extra pounds, if only to spare other guests the possible sight of a half-naked drunk struggling to the toilet in the middle of the night.

When Anne Marie, the lady of the house, had accepted me as a guest on her premises, she had been affable enough, but when I began to wheel my fridge up the front path and she discovered the true nature of my identity, her demeanour altered and I was confronted with an insanely grinning woman.

'My God, it's *you*! They've been telling people to look out for you on North West Radio. Well done, you made it to Sligo, then.'

Apparently so.

'Come in and have a cup of tea.'

I smiled at Antoinette who looked back at me resignedly.

'Okay, I have faith in the fridge,' she said, rather magnanimously.

was reaching a point in my journey where I was beginning to become aware that something special was happening to me. There were lessons and signposts almost everywhere I looked. Take the initial exchange with the man in the delicatessen for example:

'What's that?'

'It's a duck egg.'

'How much is it?'

'What do you want a duck egg for?'

'I don't know, I just like the look of it. How much is it?'

'Don't be so silly, you don't want a duck egg.'

'I do. I want to buy this duck egg off you.'

'No, now come on, what would you want with a duck egg?'

This shopkeeper had not embraced the concept of an aggressive hard sell. Far from it. In fact he saw his role as being someone who sold his goods only to those who would really benefit from them. Somehow the shopkeeper sensed from my manner that I was not a serious duck-egg purchaser. (To this day I'm still not exactly sure as to what kind of person would fall into that category, but I do know that the shopkeeper was right in divining that it wasn't me.) I look on this man now as being rather heroic. He clearly didn't see his job in terms of how much money he had made by the end of each day, but instead by how much of a service he had been able to offer. He was there to provide duck eggs to people who would make good use of them – and the same could no doubt be said for the rest of his produce.

The attitude of the shopkeeper seemed a far cry from the culture I had left behind in busy London, where most people gave the impression that they were running around trying to sell as much of whatever they could to whomever they could for the highest price the market would allow. If it entered into the equation at all, service didn't seem to be the priority.

I wondered how that old man in the deli would have managed were he required to work in the cut-throat world of sales.

'How many of our state-of-the-art TVs did you sell this month?' his manager might ask at their monthly meeting.

'None.'

'None?'

'That's right, none. Everyone I visited already had a television that seemed to work well enough so I had a nice cup of tea and a chat instead of trying to sell them another.'

This idea – that we can offer a service to others and, more importantly, that this should be our *motivation* – has all but disappeared from so many walks of life. Is the doctor more preoccupied with creating a profitable practice or with healing? Are schools more concerned with exam results and league tables than with helping to produce young people who are happy and balanced and eager to make a contribution? Are food manufacturers making food to keep us healthy or to provide wealth for their shareholders?

'Duck Egg Man' had helped to explain what our direction needs to be.

Find out how you can best be of service –
and then get on with it.

Being of service doesn't mean you have to be saving babies in the Third World. It just means making a contribution, and there are many ways in which we can do that. The postman delivers letters, the plumber ensures we get water from our pipes, the policeman protects (one would hope!) and the delicatessen provides us with duck eggs (if we're lucky). When these people recognise the value of what they are doing, their self-esteem goes up and they feel happier. Then they are able to give an even better service. Everybody wins.

Some of us might be wondering whether, in the job we do, we're actually being of any service. Perhaps we work for a global organisation and we feel like a tiny cog in a huge wheel. Maybe we feel like all we're doing is helping to make the boss rich. Perhaps we don't even like our job. In these cases, until we can find a job that will be more fulfilling, we may need to look further than our work to find out how we can be of service. It may be that it is enough to be kind to someone or to offer a sympathetic ear when required. Perhaps it would be enough to go into work making our focus being kind to all of the people around us, and not allowing one negative comment to spill from our lips.

Perhaps it's enough of a service to be a *positive influence*. The interesting thing is that the biggest beneficiary will most likely be you.

IT'S FRIDAY NIGHT ...

'So, are you going to take the fridge out tonight?' asked Antoinette after we'd all had a nice cup of tea at Anne Marie's guesthouse.

'What?' I replied. 'Are you suggesting I take it to the pub?'

'Well, it's Friday night. You can hardly leave it in on its own.'

And so it was that half an hour later, Antoinette having postponed meeting some friends who lived in the area, we opened the door and proudly marched into the Strand, the heads of those at the bar turning towards me in unison, as if following the flight of a tennis ball at Wimbledon. A man with a beard who was enjoying a quiet drink with his girlfriend looked down at the fridge. His face lit up and his eyes sparkled like those of a child at Christmas.

'Well, if it isn't the man with the fridge!'

He offered his hand, and I duly shook it and said, 'Hello, my name's Tony. This is Antoinette.'

He nodded and turned to his lady friend. 'Mary, have you heard about this fella? He's bringing a fridge round Ireland.'

'Jeez, what an eejit. What's he drinking?'

My new 'friends', Willy and Mary, took us under

their wing and introduced us to everyone they knew in the pub. With frightening predictability, I was involved in another 'session', with drinks, conversation and hospitality flowing like floodwater. Among the enthusiastic gathering who were now around me, I noticed a big man with blond hair tied in a ponytail, eyeing me with interest. He waited for the initial hubbub to subside and then approached me, full jug of lager held proudly aloft before him.

'I've heard about what you're up to and I just wanted to congratulate you.'

'Oh thanks.' I thought for a moment. 'What for?'

'Look around you. Everyone is having a damn good laugh about you and your fridge. You may not know it, but you're spreading joy.'

I was in the company of Peter, whose loose-fitting clothes of a predominantly reddish-pink hue led me to believe he was something of a buddhist. We talked, laughed, bought each other pints, and it soon became clear that we were coming at life from exactly the same direction. I knew as little about his faith as I did about my own, but he clearly *understood* what the fridge journey was all about and gave it credit where I had never thought credit was due. It was nice to hear how you were 'transcending the material' from someone who had a full pint of lager and a fag on the go.

Antoinette came and joined us. She was either having the time of her life or she was trying to postpone contact with her 'friends' as long as possible.

'I'm having the time of my life,' she said, clearing that one up right away. 'I've just met Bingo. He's the manager of this place, and you'd never believe it, but I interviewed him for a TV show in 1988 after they had the storms up here. You'll meet him in a minute – he's

insisting we have meals on the house, so he'll be over with a menu.'

Bingo. A great name, and one that in my present circumstances it seemed appropriate to shout. My numbers were most definitely coming up.

Antoinette fell under Peter's spell.

'He's wise, isn't he?' I whispered to her, and as I did so he demonstrated his wisdom with a visit to the lavatories to create more space for lager.

'He's certainly got a calmness about him,' said Antoinette. 'And there are some questions about his philosophy I want to ask.'

'But what about your friends—'

It was too late, she had fallen victim to a stealthy advance from Michael and was now beginning the smiling and nodding that a conversation with him involved. Michael was *almost* the Strand's drunk in residence, fulfilling all the criteria required but for the fact that he was mobile. Though shaky on his feet, he was still able to move freely about the pub and ensnare innocent drinkers, offering a long-winded, barely intelligible and uninformed opinion on absolutely any subject. Antoinette's eyes glazed over and, with laudable disloyalty, I sidled off, smirking.

Leaving it long enough to make it look like I wasn't copying Peter's idea, I set off for the toilets. It was a good forty minutes before I made it back, interest in my fridge adventure apparently having gripped the pub's entire clientele, and I felt obliged to offer each well-wisher a certain amount of time. It would have been churlish to do otherwise, and I soon resembled a kind of Prince Charles-lite, doing lots of nodding and hand clasping. When I got back to Antoinette, Michael had been sidelined somehow, and Peter was in full flow.

'You see, life is little more than a dream. The world isn't a physical reality, but a three-dimensional illusion. Our left side knows this, but our right side takes the materialist view. Our left side knows that life is a chosen adventure in consciousness. We are conscious beings who have freely chosen to be physical. Consciousness didn't emerge from matter; matter emerged from consciousness.'

At this point the efficacy of his enlightened peroration was undermined by someone offering him a pint of lager. He gave the thumbs-up and mouthed the word 'Carlsberg'. Probably. He continued: 'You see, everything is interconnected – all energy, all consciousness. There are no "separate" objects or "separate" beings. Time, space and separateness are illusions. So nothing actually exists.'

As he said this, a pint of lager was passed to him, which for something that didn't exist he looked far too pleased to see.

'My fridge exists,' I said defiantly.

'Ah well, I'll not argue with that.'

We all looked at it sitting happily by the door. It had grown tolerant of its master's excesses. It was an odd place and time to discover how I was being of service, but Peter seemed to recognise it immediately.

'Look around you,' he'd said. 'Everyone is having a damn good laugh about you and your fridge. You may not know it, but you're spreading joy.'

It would have sounded somewhat conceited if I'd said it myself, but I guess Peter was right. At this moment no one could dispute the fact that my fridge and I were cheering people up. You only had to look at the faces of the people in the pub to see it.

The frivolity of this quest and the incongruity of a

domestic appliance as a travelling companion were raising smiles on a daily basis, and more often than not howls of laughter. The fridge and I had become joy-bringers. There was a nice symbiosis in it all too. We were being given a lift by drivers – and in return we were providing a lift of our own: in spirits.

We human beings tend to feel good when we're laughing. Scientists have worked out that laughter releases all kinds of endorphins that are beneficial to our health and general wellbeing. Most of us know we feel good when we have a good chuckle; we recognise that we need laughter in our lives. Some of it we can provide for ourselves, and for some we look to others. These 'others' – be they comedians, writers, clowns or actors – are providing a much-needed service.

So that was it. I was providing a service by being a conduit for laughter and light relief. Better still, in the course of all this I was also having experiences that were awakening me to all that I'm writing now in this book. And just to complete the circle I'm passing on those discoveries to you – and hopefully being of service again.

Passing stuff on is exactly what I should be doing. Years ago another hitch-hiking trip had taught me that, and I was simply being reminded of it on this journey.

The first time I ever hitch-hiked in my life was in North America in the 1980s. It went well. In one triumphant day I made it all the way from Toronto to New York City – in a fraction of the time it would have taken me on the Greyhound Bus. One of my drivers, perhaps noticing how undernourished I appeared to be, insisted on buying me a huge lunch. When I thanked him for his generosity, he simply said, 'Pass it on.' This seemed very selfless – repay *me* by rewarding *someone else entirely.* I like it. It fits perfectly with the adage of 'What goes around comes around.' Put good energy out there and somehow good energy will come back to you. This may be a concept that is difficult to measure or to prove scientifically but it is surprising how many people accept that there is truth in it. It's almost as if we *know* this instinctively.

Pass it on.

Try it. The next time someone does something kind or generous to you, thank them – but instead of fretting about what present to buy them or how to make recompense, simply make a decision that you'll behave similarly to someone else the next time the opportunity arises. (And don't get upset if the receiver of your kindness doesn't show you enough 'gratitude'. Do it without expecting anything in return, knowing that you will benefit long-term in ways that cannot be measured.)

I think the onus is on us to pass things on. That way we ensure there is positive energy flowing around, and good things will come to us. Amazingly, giving and sharing will provide *more* for us.

It's almost as if we should all indulge in a kind of *enlightened selfishness* – give more away in order to get more back.

A SUITABLE WAVE

The Friday night was to produce more than just Peter's wisdom and the beginning of my understanding why I was making this absurd trip. It was to sow the seed for one of the more surreal incidents in my life.

Antoinette had had the wisdom to leave the pub early and join the friends with whom she was going to spend the night. Foolishly I remained in the pub, which closed at around 1 a.m. There seemed to be no effort on the part of the management to remove me. I had survived some kind of arbitrary selection process and was one of the drinkers privileged to be part of a lock-in. Other survivors included Michael, the resident drunk, and Peter – who was now discussing surfing with the pub's manager.

'I've never tried surfing. Can you do it here in Strandhill?' I asked.

'The beach here in Strandhill is excellent for it,' said Peter. 'Bingo here is a champion surfer; if you ask him nicely, he'll take you out surfing tomorrow.'

Bingo didn't need to be asked nicely.

'Ah sure, Tony, we'll get you a wetsuit and we'll have you up on a board within an hour.'

'Really?'

'I'll guarantee it.'

Michael had been observing this with some interest. Now was the moment for his contribution.

'Of course, you'll have to take the fridge.'

We all looked at him as if we hadn't just heard what we had just heard. But oh yes, we had, because there was more.

'Tony, you can't go surfing and not let your fridge have a go. If you surf, the fridge has to surf – it would be unfair otherwise.'

There was a pause while this sank in. Then Peter looked at Bingo.

'Could you get a fridge on a board?'

He thought for a moment.

'Yes, I think it's possible.'

Suddenly everyone became animated on the subject of the plausibility of taking a fridge surfing. Methods for strapping it to the board and techniques for getting it far enough out past the breakers were discussed with a totally incongruous gravitas. Surely these guys didn't actually mean all this?

Morning brought the discovery that it seemed like they did.

Beside my bed was a note written in my own drunken scrawl. 'Meet Bingo at 11.00.' Of course, the surfing. Were we really going to go for it?

'Do you want a coffee?' said Bingo from his familiar position behind the bar.

'Thanks, that would be nice.'

'Where's yer fridge? I've sorted you out with a wetsuit.'

'What?'

'Well, you'll need a wetsuit in there. It's pretty cold, you know.'

'Do you mean to tell me, Bingo, that we're really going to have a go at taking the fridge surfing?'

'Of course.'

'But I thought that was all just drunken high spirits.'

'You were drunk. I wasn't. We'll do it all right. You'd better go fetch the fridge.'

Surely not. But I looked at Bingo and saw that he wasn't joking. Then I heard a female voice behind me.

'Ah, there you are!' It was Antoinette, perky and alert, a picture of abstemious freshness. She eyed me cannily. 'Tony Hawks, I hope you have left this establishment since I last saw you.'

'Oh, I had a couple of hours over the road.'

'So, what are you up to this morning?'

I looked at her, and saw a woman who had been in the company of friends. Sane, sensible, balanced individuals.

'I think you had better sit down.'

Antoinette and Bingo were perched on the beach wall giggling as I advanced towards them, the loud rattling vibrations of the fridge on its trolley compounding the intensity of an already well-established headache. It was a Saturday morning and those who had chosen to spend it enjoying a pleasant beachside walk were understandably bemused by the unusual sight before them.

Surfing is a glamorous sport. Mention surfers to most of the girls I know and they will make a funny kind of grunting sound, which I have always taken to mean that they expect hunky, healthy and sexy men to be involved. And rightly so. Most of the TV footage of this sport that I have seen has involved hunky, healthy and sexy men in abundance. But there are two simple ways to take the glamour out of surfing. The first is to wear a wetsuit that is a size too small for you, and the second is to bring a fridge along. I was doing both. To be fair to Bingo, he did look the part, but he suffered by association. There was no doubting that he was *with* the bloke who looked very stupid and was carrying a fridge, and it was difficult to be truly sexy if you kept that kind of company.

We set off from the beach wall on our journey to the sea's edge. This involved us walking along the promenade and then clambering over some rocks before reaching the vast expanses of open sandy beach. The wetsuit was getting tighter and tighter round me, and I was finding it increasingly difficult to bend my limbs. The effect of this was to diminish still further my overall sexiness. I was moving like a monster from a 1930s horror movie, the only clue for observers that I wasn't such a creature being the presence of a brilliant white kitchen appliance, which was clearly one of the more recent models on the market.

When I nearly fell over, Bingo, in a big-hearted gesture, gave me his surfboard and took over the burden of the fridge, thus relinquishing any 'beach cred' he may have still had. I was now able to observe for myself just how ridiculous a man in a wetsuit carrying a refrigerator really looked. As we started clambering, I could see a small crowd gathering by the beach wall in wonderment.

The conditions were by no means ideal for surfing, the sea being altogether too calm, but this probably favoured the fridge, which was new to all this and hadn't been designed with this kind of activity in mind.

'What's the plan, then?' I said to Bingo as we began wading out to sea.

'I think what we'll do is balance the fridge on the board, and then I'll try and jump on with it and ride in on a wave.'

'Good idea,' I lied, and held the board steady as he lifted the fridge on to it.

It looked surprisingly stable on the board, a fridge's well-placed centre of gravity being one of its strong points. However, its ability to adjust it in the face of a wave is not, and unfortunately the first wave to come its way was quite large in stature. Despite his prowess in the realm of surfboarding, Bingo had no experience in the art of keeping a fridge balanced on one, and as the wave suddenly forced the board upwards, he lost his grip on the fridge and it slid sideways into the sea. Fortunately, it just remained afloat long enough for Bingo and me to dive towards it and reinstate its position above the salt water. That had been a close one. If it fell in again and we failed to get to it quickly enough, it might fill with water and sink, and the weight of the water within it would make it difficult or even impossible to raise without professional underwater lifting equipment. Foolishly, I hadn't packed any professional underwater lifting equipment.

If I was to lose the fridge in such a way as this, it would make for a difficult explanation as a reason for failure to win my bet: 'Well, it all went very smoothly indeed until I reached Strandhill and I had a touch of bad fortune when the fridge sank just off the coast, and we were unable to raise it.'

If the fridge did sink, it would also be a consider-able inconvenience to bathers, who would have to learn the exact position of the wrecked fridge or risk the agony of their toes ramming into its rusting metal shell. In the future, it might even appear on naval charts of these waters, novitiate navigators baffled by the small white cuboid marked as a hazard just off the shore.

We lifted the fridge back on to the board and Bingo pushed the two of them further out to sea, this time paying more attention to oncoming waves. I watched him as he waded out a good distance, my camera poised ready to capture this lunacy on film. He turned and waited, watching each wave in anticipation of his moment. Suddenly a bigger wave appeared and Bingo leapt on his board to join the fridge. The most extraordinary sight followed. A man and a fridge riding the waves in perfect harmony. For a few glorious yards the two of them coasted in with such ease that Bingo looked to have time to open the fridge door and take out a refreshing drink. The onlookers on the promenade broke into a spontaneous round of applause, and from the water's edge Antoinette cheered gamely. It had been done, the fridge had surfed, and what is more I had photographic evidence. Okay, the surfers hadn't exactly covered a huge distance, and it hadn't been long before Bingo had needed to leap off the board quickly and save the fridge from another drenching, but nonetheless for a matter of seconds it had been a magnificent victory for Man and Domestic Appliance over the turbulent and untamed sea.

'Congratulations, Bingo, I think that's a first,' I said.

'Thanks. The trick now is to get the thing coming in on its own.'

'Eh?'

'We've got to get the fridge to surf on its own.'

Have we? Why? Honestly, with these people if it wasn't one thing, it was another. Here was me, innocently trying to hitch round Ireland with a fridge, and I kept running into people who wanted to find all kinds of new and exciting things for the fridge to do.

'Oh, all right,' I said cravenly. 'What's the best way to do that, then?'

'Well, what I propose is that you wait about here and I'll wade a bit further out, and when I see a wave that looks suitable, I'll give the board a shove and with any luck the fridge will ride in on the board until you catch it.'

What could be simpler?

The whoops, hollers and applause we received from the shore were entirely deserved.

'We'd better not do it again,' I said. 'It would never go as well as that again. Ever.'

It had gone like a dream, exactly as Bingo had planned, the solitary fridge riding in on the wave and the surfboard arriving on cue before my outstretched arms as if guided there by remote control. And what a sight it had been. Surreal, funny and somehow inspiring. For the benefit of a crowd of about fifteen people who wouldn't be believed when they got home, the kind of stunt you might expect to see in a big-budget movie had been carried out for nothing by a couple of jokers.

'You guys are something else,' said Antoinette as we came ashore, delivering a line that could have been lifted directly from the movie in which our stunt belonged.

But we weren't just 'something else' – we were 'somewhere else' too. We were in a place of silliness and joy. A place of fun and laughter. A place of complete happiness.

But how did I get there? Why was this happening to me?

When I bade my farewells to Bingo, Peter, Antoinette and the rest of the cast and crew of this bizarre production, it was like saying goodbye to old friends, in spite of the fact I'd only met them the day before. Was it just good fortune that I was running into these amazing, generous and fun people – or was something else at work here?

I now think that what was happening was being created by the positive energy surrounding this whole 'fridge-hiking' experience. I know this may sound a little 'New Agey' or like I've turned into some kind of 1960s hippy, but bear with me for a moment.

Once I'd overcome the hurdles of the first morning's hitching, I'd been on something of a roll. As a result, my mind had shifted gear and seemed to be locked into a line of thinking that was uncompromisingly positive. The more it remained that way, the more good things continued to happen. It was like magic – except that it wasn't magic, it was very simple and it's what happens to us all when we use our thoughts wisely and constructively. Our thoughts and mood influence the events that unfold around us.

How much others help us is directly related to the mood we are in. It's generally claimed that a dog only bites someone who is afraid of it. We all know instances of a 'bad atmosphere' hanging in the air. We've all been in a room after there's been an argument and sensed the pervading mood. Could it be that there's an energy we create around us which acts as a kind of signal to other people, and influences how they react to us?

If so, then we're giving out signals all day just through our demeanour even though we might not realise it. The responses to this are helping to dictate what happens to us as our day unfolds. A negative thought, particularly one that we hold on to, could be having a much greater influence on what comes to pass in our lives than we ever imagine. It's probably acting as a huge obstacle to some of the positive things that we'd like to happen to us.

The hugely successful hitch that I recounted earlier, from Toronto to New York in a day, was quite possibly the success it was because I'd had only positive thoughts in my head. It was only after the event that someone had informed me that hitch-hiking in North America was very dangerous. My obliviousness to the danger had somehow made me immune to it. Innocence is indeed bliss.

Our thoughts are incredibly powerful. Here's a little test you might like to try with a friend, which bears this out.

Ask your friend to prepare two things that they will be able to focus their thoughts on when asked to do so. One should be overwhelmingly positive in nature, and the other very negative. (For example, the positive thought might be a wonderful day out with friends, and the negative thought might be the horrors or atrocities of war.) Then you explain that you are going to ask them to hold their arms up at their sides so they are standing like a scarecrow, and when they are in position you will push down on their arms while they try to resist you. Now they know what you are going to do, you ask them to begin thinking of one of their two 'thoughts' – but they shouldn't tell you which of the two they choose. When they are ready, and focused on their thought, ask them to put their arms up. Then you step forward and push down on their arms. You will feel how much resistance is there. Get them to relax for another moment before asking them to start focusing on the other thought. When they are ready, repeat the procedure.

In my experience, nine times out of ten you are instantly able to tell when your friend was thinking the negative thoughts because the resistance in their arms is so much weaker. With some people the difference in resistance is quite dramatic.

For me, this is excellent evidence that goes some way to proving the power of thought. Negative and positive thoughts are impacting immediately on our physical body. You are stronger when you are more positive. It's also quite probable, although it isn't so simple to prove, that your positive and negative thoughts are also impacting on the way people around you behave, thus changing your reality.

On my fridge-hiking trip I definitely got on a kind of 'positive high'. There were some days when the fridge and I felt invincible. This must have affected how everyone reacted to us. The same is true of you. If you are upbeat, laughing and joking and showing an interest in other people, it is far more likely that they will make positive suggestions or offer you assistance. Doors begin to open. If you are grumpy and uncommunicative, the chances are that those around will withdraw and not offer much help.

I am responsible for creating my own happiness.

Once you've realised this, even if you lose a friend, a lover, a job or an opportunity, you will know that you possess the power to create something joyful to fill the void. If you are living and thinking in the right way, then you will be attracting what you need. Knowing that you are the creator of your happiness will give you the reassurance and the self-confidence to be able to cherish the love of others while being able to return it with a love that is more pure, and without dependency or conditions.

You'll feel confident that what you 'give out' will have a direct and immediate effect on what you 'get back' from others. You'll start to experience things that people call 'good luck'. But is it good luck? Maybe the people we call 'lucky' aren't lucky at all, they're just experts, unwittingly maybe, at emitting positive energy. That's why the expression 'You make your own luck' is entirely accurate. And lucky people are happy people.

RAINFOREST

Before I left Strandhill and said goodbye to my newfound friends, Bingo had another activity planned.

'You've got to see the Glen,' said Bingo. 'You can't leave here without seeing the Glen.'

'What's the Glen?'

'You'll see. You've got a car, Antoinette, haven't you? It'll only take us half an hour.'

And so the relentless programme of events continued with a visit to the Glen. Neither Antoinette nor I had any idea what it was, but we had been assured we shouldn't leave this place without seeing it, and as two followers of the 'faith', we knew it would be wrong to let the opportunity pass.

Bingo must have had second thoughts when he saw Antoinette's car. He said nothing but his expression suggested that his thought was, 'And you want me to get *in* it?'

In the past, Bingo had given detailed directions to holidaymakers but none of them had managed to find the Glen. It was like a secret place, not in any guide-books and accessible only to a select few who were in the know. After ten minutes of driving, the road started to carve its way round a hill, giving us views across the beautiful bays and inlets of the coast on our right-hand side, and steep grassy banks on the other.

'Right, just pull over on the left here,' said Bingo.

He led us across the road where there was a tiny gate almost completely hidden by overgrown bushes and long grass.

'This is it.'

A short walk down a narrow path and we were in a place that was truly special. Like three children on an adventure, we found ourselves descending into a narrow passage at the foot of two huge walls of stone. There were two theories about what had caused this vast fault in the limestone rock around the time of the Ice Age: an earthquake, or the top collapsing in on an underground river. We were now the fortunate witnesses to the spectacular result. Vegetation growing over the rock face and water trickling over limestone stalactites had created, in microcosm, Sligo's very own tropical rainforest. The narrow shafts of light battling through the overhanging branches and leaves, the sound of running water and the echoes of our voices gave the place a mystical quality that required us to stop talking and just listen. Listen to the voice of Nature.

I walked on ahead, sat down on a tree stump and looked up at the huge limestone walls that encased and sheltered us. As I watched the youthful water of a mini waterfall cascading over a narrow strip of stone, I allowed its gentle sounds to send me into a faintly meditative state. A rare moment of peace in a journey that had become a hectic and clamorous celebration of the absurd. I felt suddenly grateful for all that had happened to me and I looked up and gently whispered, 'Thank you.' This was directed to no one and nothing

in particular, but to anyone or anything who was listening and fancied taking the credit. I looked around me and saw that both Bingo and Antoinette had found their own private locations for a moment's quiet contemplation, and I felt deeply privileged to be here in this unique and spiritual place.

By accident we had stumbled upon the very important activity of inactivity.

Slow down and create some moments of peace.

Some days it just feels like we're rushing everywhere. However, if we're in a hurry, then we might be missing out on so many things simply because we don't have the time to see them. Had I been in a rush to resume my journey after the fridge surfing, then I would have missed out on the Glen and a special moment of peace.

One of the big advantages of hitch-hiking is that being in a hurry simply doesn't work. It would drive you mad. The erratic nature of this method of travel means that the hitcher needs to put his trust in his thumb and just wait patiently for help to come along. You have to accept that stuff might not happen as quickly as you'd like. However, quite often there is some value in the time that we are required to wait, although we might not recognise it at the time.

Waiting can be a positive thing. If we use it wisely it can offer us a period of reflection. A chance to assess, analyse, and then perhaps make a wiser, more informed choice. For much of our lives we're rushing from one thing to another. This isn't necessarily the best way of doing things.

There were times on my fridge journey when it all became exhausting. The nature of hitch-hiking is that you need to engage in dialogue with the person who has given you the lift. It's not considered good form simply to go to sleep as soon as you flop down into the passenger seat. Your 'job' is to help the driver by offering friendly conversation and making their journey a little more fun. However, there were times when I wanted nothing more than to go to sleep. Instead I had to answer the barrage of questions:

'Is that a fridge?'

'What on earth would anyone be doing travelling with a fridge?'

'Jeez, I heard about you on the radio. Great stuff! But tell me – why a fridge?'

It wasn't as if things were any easier when I arrived at my bed and breakfast or guesthouse:

'Is that a fridge?'

'What on earth would anyone be doing travelling with a fridge?'

'Jeez, I heard about you on the radio. Great stuff! But tell me – why a fridge?'

Then when I went out for a drink or a bite to eat:

'Is that a fridge?'

'What on earth would anyone be doing travelling with a fridge?'

'Jeez, I heard about you on the radio. Great stuff! But tell me – why a fridge?'

In the end I came to treasure the moments when I was just waiting for a lift. I came to see that the time I spent standing peacefully by the roadside or sitting quietly on my fridge wasn't wasted time – it was offering me valuable rest and the opportunity to make some sense of all the things that were happening around me.

So, we can wait patiently for help to arrive. After all, what's the hurry anyway? If the journey is all you have, then what's the point of hurrying to the final destination? We need to recognize that it is in our interests to find time to slow down.

Our lives are journeys. If we rush everywhere, then we may miss out on the fine views along the way. The beauty of hitch-hiking is that you can never rush. It's almost as if you make a deal with yourself before you start – *this will take as long as it takes*. Not a problem. Be there when you get there.

At some point or other we've all read a book that we were enjoying so much we didn't want it to finish. When that happens we don't speed-read it, or skip passages. No, we savour every chapter, every paragraph, every word. So are we savouring enough of our lives? Or is life speeding past us, slightly out of control? Are we failing to take in the beauty that is all around us?

If the end of our journey is Dublin, and the completion of the journey is the end of our lives, then why would we be in a hurry to get to Dublin?

Ireland offered me further wisdom when I returned there later to make a short publicity tour promoting the publication of *Round Ireland with a Fridge*. One day I stopped my hire car and asked directions from an old man who was standing at the side of the road, looking to be anything but a man who was in a hurry. He explained to me that there were two possible routes I could take to get to my destination. The first was by way of a scenic mountain lane and the second required me to continue along the main road.

'The mountain route is actually further in terms of kilometres,' he explained, 'but I think it's quicker because it's more beautiful.'

f waiting can be a positive opportunity for reflection, then my hitch out of Strandhill was extremely kind to me. I was hoping to get to Ballina, but I was still by the roadside an hour and a half after I'd begun, with my thumb raised slightly less optimistically than at the outset. With an overconfidence that was perhaps now bordering on arrogance, I had thought that I could just leave a town whenever I felt like it and pick up a lift with great ease. The reality was that in another hour it would be dark and I would have to give up and get a taxi back to Strandhill. Could my liver handle another night in the pub with my fridge-surfing entourage? I slumped down on to the fridge, my mood very much at the cusp of a downturn.

Two very young children, a little boy and a little girl, walked past. The boy viewed me with some interest and asked, 'What are you doing?'

It was a question I had begun to ask myself.

'I'm hitch-hiking.'

He nodded. He seemed satisfied even though he clearly didn't know what 'hitch-hiking' was.

'Are you just after coming from school?' the little girl asked.

I shook my head, more in disbelief than in answer to the question. What cross-circuit of wires in her brain had caused her to arrive at a question like that? I looked like a lot of things, but the one thing I did not resemble was a child. Or was fridge hitch-hiking so outside the sphere of a normal adult's activities that to this girl a child was all I could possibly be?

Finally a car stopped. But the driver got out and crossed the road to the convenience store.

Tease.

For the next ten minutes all the drivers seemed to be solitary lady drivers, and for obvious reasons solitary lady drivers don't stop. Especially on a Saturday night and when the hitcher has a fridge. A priest went by, but he made a signal with his hand, pointing to the left, meaning that he was turning off very shortly. Quite a few drivers had done this and I respected it as a courteous gesture, even if nine times out of ten it was probably a downright lie.

Another twenty minutes dragged by. Clutching at straws, I decided what I was lacking was a card to hold up with my destination written on it. Up until now I hadn't bothered with this hitch-hiking accessory since I had no real need for one. It didn't matter particularly where I ended up: any kind of lift, provided it was in roughly the right direction, was good enough for me. The nice lady in the convenience store provided me with a piece of cardboard, and after a little creative work with the marker pen I went back to my hitching with renewed vigour, and with a 'BALLINA' sign held proudly aloft.

It didn't make a scrap of difference. Well, it did, actually: now the drivers knew exactly where it was they weren't going to take me. It was almost half past seven. I decided twenty more minutes and then I would give up and call for a taxi to take me back to Anne Marie's. Three unsavoury-looking youths turned the corner and headed towards me. For the first time on my trip I felt a little uneasy. It was Saturday night, they looked a tough lot, and I was something of a target for those in search of alternative amusement. Would they say anything? Worse still, would they do anything? I held my breath and closed my eyes, but they passed by without a word. Quite whether I was all too confusing a proposition for them, or whether they were simply law-abiding, upstanding citizens, I do not know. Perhaps the fridge made me look hard.

I was about to give up, and had just started to gather my irregular belongings together when a Vauxhall Cavalier pulled up. I watched it suspiciously, expecting the driver to get out and go across to the store, but he remained in his seat and looked over his shoulder at me. I ran to the car window.

'Are you going to Ballina?' I asked.

'I am too.'

I had lucked out again.

'YOU'VE PROBABLY HEARD HIM ON *THE GERRY RYAN SHOW*'

Just like Andy had done in Bunbeg, Marjorie offered me free accommodation in her B&B in Ballina. When I thanked her for her kindness she made her position clear.

'Think nothing on it, Tony. When I heard what you were doing I just had to ring the radio station and offer you a room. I think it's a great idea.'

Of course it was. I had never doubted it.

I explained that I wanted to have a little rest before I went and explored Ballina's nightlife, and at 8.30 I got my head down for an hour's nap.

When I awoke from the deepest of sleeps it was only 8.45. I got up to go to the toilet and looked out of the bathroom window. I saw the sun shining on the river. From the east. It was morning. I had napped for twelve and a quarter hours. And I felt rather good for it.

'Did you sleep all right?' asked Marjorie, at breakfast.

'You could say that.'

Having taken note of my choice of breakfast, Marjorie shuffled off, leaving me to admire the view of the river and chat to the other guests. I surveyed them and elected not to bother. There were three of them – a young married couple and a lone, obese German man – and they were all sat at one table together and clearly not having a very comfortable time. They were saying absolutely nothing to each other and their silence seemed to have a terrible stranglehold over them. The sound of their cutlery clinking on their crockery echoed round the dining room and seemed to be amplified tenfold. It became apparent that for all of them the task of introducing words into the proceedings was becoming increasingly hard with each passing minute. They hung their heads over their plates with grim determination and resolve, knowing that the sooner their food was eaten, the sooner the whole unpleasant experience would be over. I was glad I wasn't sat at their table.

Marjorie's voice seemed deafening when she arrived with the most wonderful plate of breakfast. Over tea, the previous day, she had told me that she had written two cookbooks, and even with as simple a meal as breakfast, she clearly wanted to demonstrate her skill in the culinary field. I had no objections: smoked salmon, tomato and beautiful fluffy scrambled egg suited me just fine. As far as I was concerned, she fully deserved the Michelin star she had told me she craved. But what's the big deal there? I have never understood the need to have one's cuisine endorsed by Michelin. Who cares what they think? No one is looking for food that corners well.

After the young couple and the now even more obese German had fled the dining room for the sanctuary of their bedrooms, Marjorie explained how she and her husband had separated, and how she felt she was starting over again and was more positive than ever about the future.

'I'm going for it!' she said. 'I think that's why I knew I had to make contact with you, because with what you're doing, you're going for it too.'

'Right.'

I knew what she meant, but I had never expected my fridge journey to be used in comparison with recovery from a marriage break-up.

'So, are you taking that fridge back out on the road today, Tony?'

'Well, Sunday is traditionally a day of rest, and I think I may have been overdoing it a little, so would you mind if I stayed here one more night – I fully expect to pay.'

'You'll do no such thing, you'll stay here for nothing and there'll be no argument about it. So, what are you going to do with your day today then?'

'Oh, I think I'll just take it easy, do some reading and writing, maybe take a walk down by the river.'

'Oh. My friend Elsie is coming over at one o'clock. She's a character – you just *have* to meet her. I'll warn you, though, you might need a Valium.'

Marjorie hadn't exaggerated. Elsie, an effervescent and voluble woman, cut short my leisure time when she arrived an hour early, and marked midday by planting a big wet smacker full on my lips.

'You'll have to excuse me, Tony, but that's the way I do things,' she spluttered as I reeled back in shock. 'Did I come too early?'

'No, you're fine, I'd nearly finished reading.'

Elsie wasn't slow in coming forward. Within two minutes of our having met, she showed me a poem she had written and asked me to read it. As I endeavoured to do so, she continued to talk, telling me how she wrote and sang songs too and was making a CD soon. Unfortunately, Elsie's incessant spoken word meant that concentration on her written word was impossible.

'It's very good,' I said, handing the poem back and hoping she wouldn't wish me to comment on its subject matter.

After a delicious lunch, which I could only fault in its alarming proximity to breakfast, the two ladies took me on a tour of the sights of Ballina. The fridge had to come too, and at all points along the way, at Elsie's and Marjorie's insistence, the fridge was to be paraded as a celebrity for all to see.

We visited Kilcullen's Seaweed Baths in Enniscrone where I had the privilege of having seaweed draped all over me while being immersed in an enormous bath of hot seawater. It seemed a ludicrous idea but was surprisingly relaxing. We dropped in at Belleek Castle, a stately home set in a thousand acres of woodland and forestry on the banks of the River Moy, but we couldn't look round it because viewings of the castle were by appointment only. That's what estate agents say, isn't it? We were hardly going to buy the place.

On the way back, a drink was taken in the clubhouse of the golf club where the ladies had begun taking lessons. I was to learn a lesson here too. As I wheeled the fridge into the bar on its trolley, Elsie announced at the top of her voice, 'THIS IS TONY HAWKS FROM ENGLAND! HE'S BRINGING A FRIDGE ROUND IRELAND! YOU'VE PROBABLY HEARD HIM ON *THE GERRY RYAN SHOW*.'

Elsie's announcement was greeted with silence. The relaxing golfers eyed me with suspicion and returned to their conversations. Marjorie, Elsie and myself drank our drinks without one person coming over to talk to us or have a joke about the fridge.

Throughout the afternoon Elsie kept up a constant stream of jokes and ribald remarks, each of the latter followed by the apology, 'I am sorry about that, but that's the way I am.'

In fact, she said 'I am sorry about that, but that's the way I am' so many times that I began to wonder whether that wasn't the way she was at all. Whatever she was, she was a good friend to Marjorie.

'A while ago now when I was low,' said Marjorie, when Elsie was out of earshot, 'I called Elsie eight times in one day. And when I called the eighth time, she behaved just like it was the first. Now *that's* a friend.'

Or someone with a very poor memory.

I felt inspired by Marjorie and Elsie. Marjorie with her cookbooks, and Elsie with her poems and songs. I had no idea whether either of their efforts were of a high quality, but that didn't seem to be the point. Far more pertinent was the joy it was bringing to them. Two women who were going for it.

What had happened back in that golf clubhouse was at odds with the rest of the trip, but it wasn't until a few days later that I worked it out. I felt sure this hadn't been the customary frostiness of golf clubs we'd experienced, but more of an example of 'Irish Begrudgery'. I remembered someone in the pub in Bunbeg announcing this alleged national trait, and I understood it to mean that people would have little time for you if you forced yourself upon them or announced your greatness, instead of allowing them their own time and space to discover it for themselves. Rightly or wrongly, the drinkers in that bar had interpreted that this is what we had done. This had changed the mood in the room and it had altered the relationship of the Fridge Man with his hosts.

The whole experience was a textbook lesson in learning the value of humility. Let people see your quality in their own time.

You don't need to show off.

What are we doing when we 'talk big' or when we try hard to create a positive impression? Aren't we simply hoping that people will like us or respect us more as a result of what we've boasted about? Isn't that a sign of insecurity? The thought is: 'I'd better say something that will impress or else these people might not like me as much as I want them to.'

Quietly confident is more attractive than *stridently self-important*, although it may not provide us with instant gratification. Patience may be required, and the approval we seek may not come when we want it, or from the desired source, but it will surely come. Provided we are living our lives simply and honestly, doing our best to be of service, then all the approval we could ever need will be in one of the cars that is about to stop and pick us up.

If we remember that we are all equal in spirit, then it's a short step to understanding that we no longer need to boast, talk big or create an impression, since we don't have any need to be *better than* anyone else, just as we can recognise that nobody else is necessarily *better than* us.

I am convinced that if the Irish people had sensed that I was making my fridge journey as a stunt in order to gain attention and fame, then my experience would have been a completely different one.

And it wouldn't have been anywhere near as much fun.

A KISSABLE MOUTH

Ballina was to provide me with my first vaguely romantic interlude of the trip. I was in a place called Murphy's that happened to be full of young people. Attractive young people. Young attractive girls. I ordered a pint and allowed myself to get a little excited. I leant against the bar and scanned the room for my favourite. She wasn't hard to find. She was sat at a table in a slightly elevated section of the pub, talking with two guys. She had dark hair, big sparkling eyes and a mouth that I felt needed to be kissed. I was considering how pleasurable an experience this might be when she looked up and saw me looking at her. I didn't look away. She gave me a kind of half smile and went back to talking with her friends. Good. The half smile was a good sign.

Perhaps at this point I should take a moment to explain how, in the area of the pursuit of women, I have always demonstrated an exceptional adeptness for deluding myself. I have always been able to convince myself that I'm doing much better than I really am. With an assured grace and on gossamer wings, I fly in the face of reality, never seeing the crash landing that awaits me. On this occasion, for example, I had completely dismissed from my mind the fact that the

object of my interest was in the company of two men who, no doubt, were just as aware of the kissability of her mouth as I was.

When she left her friends (for in my eyes that was all they were) and came to the bar to order a drink, she was almost alongside me, presenting me with an opportunity I couldn't afford to miss. However, I made the mistake of thinking too much about the opening line. By far and away the best option in this situation is to say the first thing that comes into your head and not worry about its quality – the thinking being that if the girl likes the general look of you, she will be moderately forgiving in the first few minutes of your advances.

Her transaction at the bar was nearly completed and I knew I had to say something, and fast.

'Is there a pub quiz on tonight?' I blurted, averting my eyes from the sign saying 'PUB QUIZ TONIGHT', which was up on the wall directly in front of both of us.

'Yes,' she replied warmly. 'You can come and be in our team if you like.'

Inwardly I punched the air, while on the cool exterior I attempted to give the impression of being rather blasé about the whole idea.

'If you like,' I said, and then, thinking I'd overdone it, added, 'Thanks, that would be nice.'

Her name was Rosheen (which I later learned was spelt 'Roisin'), and she wasn't with the two guys at the table, but with a crowd of friends who were further up the bar to my left. With great politeness, not normally afforded to a stranger who had just asked you a stupid question, she introduced me to all her friends, one by one, but their names were just sounds I failed to absorb, such was my fixation with her, the mistress of ceremonies. It mattered only that it was her name I remembered. Roisin. Lovely Roisin. With the kissable mouth.

I felt a tingle of nerves when I was at that bar alongside Roisin – and I didn't want to fail, and I didn't want to make a fool of myself. Perhaps I wouldn't have risked saying anything at all had I not been on the fridge journey, and my confidence and positive energy hadn't been quite as high. The fear, and that's what I was feeling, was unfounded (as it so often is) because Roisin was friendly and welcoming and very soon I was invited to join her and her friends. New doors were opening up to me.

Of course, had I spent even longer before I'd blurted out the brilliant line 'Is there a pub quiz on tonight?* then I might have ended up saying nothing as I auditioned each line and rejected it.

There is an argument to suggest that our fears can *attract* the very thing we are fearful of happening. Nerves, arising from a fear of not succeeding, can be the very cause of failure. The single person who is scared of not finding a partner often drives away a prospective partner by being overly keen or needy, for example. Sports psychology offers up further evidence to back this theory up.

My friend Paul trained to be a professional tennis player. Years ago he was Tim Henman's doubles partner and was part of the elite squad that was training for competitive tennis as a career. One day they had a session with a sports psychologist who sat all the players in a circle and asked them to imagine a match situation in which they were 8–7 ahead in the final set

---

* Feel free to use that line, guys. I'm happy to share.

and it was match point to them on their serve. They miss their first service. He explained that most players at this point would tell themselves, 'Don't double fault!' The psychologist asked how many players had told themselves exactly that at some point in their short tennis careers. Nearly all of the players put their hands up.

'And how many of you have told yourselves that, and then gone on to serve a double fault immediately afterwards?' he continued.

Again, nearly all hands went up. He explained that this was because they had been 'visualising' a double fault – and that very often what we 'visualise' actually comes to pass.

'Okay – now what I want every one of you to do,' he continued, 'when I say so, I want all of you NOT to think of the next thing that I say. Okay, here goes. I want you NOT to think of a kangaroo. Off you go.'

The sports psychologist left everyone for a moment and then asked for a show of hands from those who had thought of a kangaroo. Every hand went up. He smiled.

'Now try even harder NOT to think of a kangaroo.'

It made it even worse. Trying harder not to think of a kangaroo only made the image of the kangaroo loom even larger in the mind. The same is true of the double fault. The fear brings it to your mind and then it is hard to shake it out again.

So how do you stop the kangaroo? How do you stop the fearful thought? How do you stop the worry? Well, we've established that trying harder *not* to think about it will only bring the image bigger into your mind. According to the sports psychologist, the trick is to think of *something else* entirely.

'When I say, "Don't think of a kangaroo," you think of a giraffe,' he suggested.

The players tried this exercise and it was entirely successful. Provided that the 'thinkers' focused on *something else*, they didn't think of the image they were being asked not to think about.

So what we need to do in our lives is a version of the same thing. We need to take away the weak, defensive, fearful thought and replace it with a positive one. For the tennis player, instead of 'Don't double fault,' it's: 'Right, I'm going to serve a big kicking second serve down the middle to my opponent's backhand.'

A few years back I was in a play at the Belgrade Theatre, Coventry. It had been a long time since I'd acted on the stage and I found myself feeling scared about forgetting my lines. On the first night I was very nervous. Fortunately, once the play began I started to relax and I performed as well as I had done in rehearsal. If I hadn't relaxed – if I had remained in a state of nerves – it would have paralysed me and ruined my performance.

Why had I been so nervous in the first place? Well, I'd been nervous because I was frightened of what would happen if I forgot my lines and stood there on the stage like an idiot in front of my fellow actors and expectant audience. Like a fool, I'd been focusing on the double fault – not the good service. I'd been putting a lot of time and energy into trying to prevent something from happening and that had only served to make the very thing I didn't want to happen a more likely occurrence.

When we're fearful we're unwittingly visualising a negative outcome. So try not to. Do the opposite.

Let go of your fears, knowing they are preventing
you from reaching your full potential.

As I continued my journey hitch-hiking round Ireland with a fridge, it became clearer what was going on. If I'd been afraid of where the next lift was going to come from – or where I was going to sleep when night fell – then my demeanour would have been completely different. An anxious expression and outlook on the world would have meant that the people I interacted with might not have made so many generous offers or offered up the opportunities to create the adventures that occurred on a daily basis. Fear of failure would have absolutely spoiled my day. And allowing every day to be spoiled would have spoiled my journey.

And why would I want to spoil that, if the journey is all I have?

PRINCESSES MERIT FLOWERS

Roisin's team didn't win the pub quiz, missing out on the winning prize by one point largely because I insisted that UB40's 'Red Red Wine' was the answer to the final question. Later, the DJ revealed all.

'.... and so we come to the final question of the night. What was Neil Diamond's first number-one hit as a writer? And the answer of course: "I'm a Believer" by the Monkees.'

I didn't look at Roisin, but apologised to the rest of my team.

'I'm sorry,' I said, with as much humility as I could muster.

'Ah, who cares?' said the fella on my left.

All was not lost. The downstairs of the pub became a nightclub after 11 p.m. and there was a further opportunity to win Roisin's affections. Soon we were in the 'disco' basement of Murphy's with all the unpleasant features I had come to associate with these places – overcrowded dance floor, booming bass, strobe lighting and mindless remarks from the DJ.

Perfect for making me feel uncomfortable. I felt I had gone back in time and was reliving one of countless unsatisfactory teenage evenings. It was a night-mare, but most of all because I had completely lost Roisin.

She was here, at least she had said she was coming, but I couldn't see her anywhere in this crowded, sweaty hellhole. Naturally, were I to bump into Roisin and find myself marching off hand in hand with her to the dance floor, I would have found the whole ambience entirely more agreeable. As it was, I was reduced to drinking beer and watching girls dancing. Man at his most atavistic.

It must have been quite close to the end of the evening when I put my pint down, marched on to the dance floor and did my little jig with as much dignity as I could muster. Nobody had asked me to dance and no one was dancing with me. I suppose this is the one advantage of the modern discotheque. Had I been doing this on my own at a 1930s dancehall, I would have been thrown out. A girl suddenly grabbed me and started swinging me about by my arms. It wasn't clear whether she was dancing with me or trying to soften me up for interrogation. Had an interrogation followed, I surely would have spilled the beans. She continued to swing me round until I was close to exhaustion. When the record finished, the lights came up, and that was it, the night was over.

Except of course that no one was in a hurry to leave. Why should they be? With the music no longer blaring, here was the first opportunity for people to talk to each other.

On my way out, I bumped into Roisin, who was in the queue for the cloakroom.

'Where have you been? I've been looking for you,' I said.

'I've been talking to Paul.'

'Who's Paul?'

'Paul is who asked me out this evening. This is our second date.'

'Oh.' I felt two hours of drink swell inside me. 'I think you're lovely, you know.'

'Do you? That's nice.' She seemed genuinely chuffed, although presumably she could spot '3 a.m. drunken boy at disco' talk when she heard it. The thing is, I really meant it.

'Do you like him?' I said.

'Who?'

'Paul – second-date man.'

She hesitated and, like a politician, chose her words carefully. 'He's a lot more local than you are.'

She had a point.

In the brief conversation that followed I broke the fridge news to her, which she assimilated with surprising ease, and then I took her address, promising to bring her flowers in the morning.

'You won't. You're just saying that,' she insisted.

'You'll see. You'll get the flowers. You're my princess and princesses merit flowers.'

I don't know whether Paul heard these last words as he arrived at his date's side, but he didn't look too pleased with me. I gave him an apologetic shrug, kissed Roisin on the hand and set off on the long walk back to my lodgings. I fell into bed, and with a ringing in my ears and a spinning of the room, wondered how long it would be before the next time I didn't sleep alone. It was like being nineteen all over again.

In the morning I decided to see it through. Martin the taxi driver agreed that it was the right thing to do.

'Ah, if you said you'd bring her flowers, then bring her flowers,' he said as he dropped me outside number 24 in a small residential estate. 'What harm can it do?'

As I rang the bell I felt a rush of nerves. I didn't know what to expect. The door opened and there was lovely Roisin, not wearing any make-up, unlike the night before, and somehow looking fresher for it. I smiled and brandished the flowers.

'Hello, remember me?'

She looked absolutely horrified. Then she put her forefinger over her mouth indicating to me to be quiet and did something that I thought only happened in poor situation comedies. For the benefit of someone inside the house, she announced to me in a loud voice, 'NO, THANK YOU, NOT TODAY – WE DON'T NEED ANY.'

Oh no! Somebody was inside who shouldn't know about me. I began to panic. God, what had I done? Perhaps last night things between her and second-date Paul had moved on apace and he was in there, having stayed the night. Perhaps he had a vicious temper, a criminal record and a penchant for brandishing things less benign than flowers. Was Martin's question on the subject of the flowers – 'What harm can it do?' – about to be comprehensively answered?

Roisin leant forward and whispered to me. Even in these uneasy circumstances, it felt good to be close to her.

'My aunt's in the house.'

Her aunt? So what? What's so special about her aunt? This was a new one on me. A jealous aunt?

Roisin must have known from the look of disbelief on my face that I was in need of elucidation.

'Look, I didn't tell you this last night, but I'm recently separated from my husband, and the family don't know about Paul, let alone ...'

'The idiot with the flowers.'

'Yes. I mean, no. Not at all. You're not an eejit.'

I bloody was. What if the husband were to turn up now? The jealous, violent psychopath of a husband.

'YES, WELL, THANK YOU. TRY AGAIN NEXT WEEK,' announced Roisin for the benefit of the aunt.

'I'd better go.'

'I'm sorry.'

This had all been rather disappointing. I handed her the flowers.

'Thank you, Tony. That's sweet.'

'Look, I've got a mobile phone, I'll give you the number, if you ever feel like giving me a call.'

'Thanks.'

'Although you're hardly likely to.'

'No, I will.' She looked me in the eye. 'I *will* call.'

Something about that look led me to believe that Roisin would call. She wasn't out of my life forever. Not just yet, anyway.

I got back into the taxi of the gently smirking Martin, leaving Roisin to explain to her aunt why a tradesman had brought her a bouquet of flowers.

'I've done a receipt for you,' said Martin, as he helped unload me and my stuff by the roadside. He handed it to me. It read:

DATE:	19th May
TO:	Dublin Road, Ballina
FROM:	Marjorie's
DRIVER'S NAME:	Martin McGurty
FARE:	£0.00

'Thanks, that's really so kind, Martin.'

Especially given the amount of his time I had taken up with stops at florists and doorstep dramas.

'I couldn't take money off the Fridge Man, now, could I?'

I couldn't argue with the logic, and was extremely grateful that this sentiment seemed to be shared by quite so many of his countrymen.

In the days that followed these events, for the first time on the trip, I began to suffer a little mentally as I anxiously waited for Roisin to call my mobile phone. She had really sounded like she was going to get in touch.

'I *will* call,' she'd said, almost with a steely determination.

She didn't, though. It didn't matter how much I sat and looked at the phone, willing her to call me, nothing happened.

This 'phone anxiety' meant that for a few days at least, I had less fun than I could have done. I 'suffered' each time I wanted Roisin to call and my phone didn't ring. I worried that she wasn't going to call at all.

Up until this point, I had begun every morning not having any clue where I was going to sleep at the end of the day, and instead of worrying about it, I had embraced the 'faith in the fridge' and made the assumption that everything would be fine. However, for a few days, something (Roisin) got to me, and I began to worry.

Let's make a list of the top ten positives of worrying:

1.

2.

3.

4.

5.

6.

7.

8.

9.

10.

In spite of the absence of any evidence of benefit, most of us indulge in worry – some of us, big time – even though people in the medical profession tell us that ultimately it leads to ill health. So why do we do it? Do we *want* to be ill? Of course not. But we just can't stop our minds from working overtime, even if we want to stop.

Of course, there's a big difference between worrying and trying to find a solution. The former involves negative thought, and the latter positive.

Most of the time when we are worrying we are trying to influence something that is beyond our control. Will I pass the exams I've just taken? Will the shares I've just bought go up in value? Will Roisin call? Will X and Y like the present I've bought them? Why have I got friends called X and Y? In all these cases I can do nothing to affect the outcome.*

One could even go as far as to argue that worry is a form of insanity. After all, how sane is it to try to

---

* With the possible exception of the last one. I could tell X and Y that I'd made some much nicer friends called T and F and that henceforth I didn't wish to see them any more.

influence something that is beyond our control? I think we would all question the sanity of someone who tried to stop the wind with their hands and push it in the opposite direction. And yet all they are trying to do is control something that is out of their control. Is the 'wind pusher' any more insane than the person who worries about whether their car will get stolen, or the students who cannot sleep because they're worried about whether they've passed their exams, or the mothers who worry about whether their children are safe when they go off on holiday with their friends? Or the hopeless fool who worries whether a girl he met for a few hours will call?

It's all a matter of recognising what you can and can't influence. We only have so much control, even over the biggest question of them all: how long are we going to live? I recall what I have heard from drinkers many times in Irish pubs over the years.

'Jeez, I might be dead next week, I'd better enjoy myself now before it's too late.'

It may be a flawed piece of wisdom, coming, as it so often does, from someone who has drunk so much that staying alive until the following week is quite an optimistic prognosis. Also, it could just be a crafty piece of manipulation to justify acting without responsibility. However, there is a profound wisdom behind this statement.

'Jeez, I might be dead next week.'

Do we not live our lives largely in denial of our own mortality? We may indeed 'be dead next week' or perhaps halfway through the week after that, but we don't like to consider the prospect. The truth is, we just don't know when we are going to pass away. Even the greatest minds on the planet are ignorant of when their moment of extinction might come. It's a mystery. However, when the moment of truth does arrive and we are able to look back over our lives, there's one thing we can be sure we won't be saying:

'You know, my biggest regret is that I didn't worry a bit more. I had so many opportunities to be more uptight about things and I just didn't take them. Oh, how I wish I had.'

There are some things about which we can do something, physically or practically. Other things we just have to do our best, get on, and wait and see. The only real influence we might have is likely to result from the quality of thought we gave to the matter. Worry is negative and harmful, while a positive thought, i.e. an active, positive, problem-solving approach, may help in some way, not least in contributing to the feeling of contentment we are all striving for.

When we worry, we suffer, but our worry provides no practical help. All it will do is spoil the day for us, and for those around us.

Worrying is not a good use of our time.

PUSHING IN

Westport was next. I'd been told at breakfast the previous day that it was a lovely little town, and that I should go to Matt Molloy's pub and get Mick Levell to sing the 'Lotto Song'. This had made absolutely no sense to me, and for that reason alone it seemed like an apposite destination.

It was a beautiful day, and my worrying period was thankfully behind me as I stuck out the thumb of destiny once more. As ever, the lift was not long in coming. Michael was a self-employed builder who was headed for Swinford. He had heard nothing about my trip before picking me up, but he thought it seemed a fun project. Incredibly enough, I'd still to meet anyone who had disapproved of this daft undertaking.

Michael dropped me at a T-junction where an arterial road from Swinford joined the main N5 road, which he told me had been built with the help of an EC grant. About half a mile up the road I could see another hitcher. I had little choice but to start hitching where Michael had dropped me, but by doing so I was effectively pushing in front of this other fellow. That didn't seem right, and it made me feel uncomfortable. No doubt I was experiencing some kind of inherited British need to play fair with regard to queuing. I think its roots are in the colonial thing. Shooting hordes of insubordinate natives was acceptable when 'needs must', but jumping a queue was *always* quite intolerable. The whole *raison d'être* for a vast British Empire was surely a desire to teach the ignorant peoples of the world how to queue correctly. We British lead the world in queuing. (Well, we used to, until a few other countries pushed in front of us.) And here was I flouting my responsibility as a good British citizen to respect this most basic of all human rights.

But what could I do? This other hitch-hiker was too far up the road for me to drag my fridge and bags over to him. Surely the onus was on him to rectify the situation. He must have been rather peeved that this other chap had pushed in front of him, but he showed no signs of marching down in my direction to protest.

This N5 was by far the best stretch of road I had come across in Ireland, but it certainly wasn't overused. Cars and lorries came along at the rate of about one a minute. This was a frustrating length of interval between vehicles. It was just long enough to feel there wasn't going to be another one along for a while and to sit down on the fridge and relax, only to find immediately I had done so that I had to jump to my feet and begin hitching again.

The N5 was to bring me a new hitching experience. Faced with the rare sight of a relatively smooth stretch of road before them, the Irish drivers clearly felt the urge to discover the maximum speed of their chosen mode of transport. This meant that the poor hitcher was only noticed at the very last minute as the driver hurtled past, and was all too soon an afterthought. Perhaps this is why the hitcher ahead hadn't protested at my arrival, calculating that the braking distance for any car that stopped for me would be such that it would draw to a halt exactly where he was standing.

I looked at my watch and saw that I had been there for over an hour. I didn't mind one bit. I was enjoying some precious time on my own. As a lone traveller I had expected a good deal more of it, but given the hectic way things were turning out, these roadside vigils were my only oases of peace.

Jack screeched to a halt. An emergency stop. Of course. If you saw the man with the fridge by the side of the road, what else was there for it? Boy, Jack was excited. He was a big fan of *The Gerry Ryan Show* and said that he had been charting my progress since day one. I climbed into the lorry's cabin, which was packed full of boxes. There was only just room to squeeze in. I looked further up the road and saw that the other hitcher was still there. He can't have been that happy, but was probably consoling himself with the fact that I would be decent enough to implore the driver to stop for him too. I would have done had there been enough room.

As we drove past him I tried to do a kind of apologetic wave, which probably backfired and looked like I was rubbing salt in the wound. She waved back. She? I looked again and saw that, yes, it was a girl. Oh no! This offended my hereditary colonial sensibilities even more. For this, I would surely be hauled before the Viceroy of the Raj.

'Now, Hawks, as you well know, we take a pretty dim view of anyone who pushes in front of the next man – but there is only one thing good enough for a man who stoops so low as to push in front of a woman. Perkins! Take him away, and have him shot.'

It wasn't until the next night that this situation resolved itself. I found myself staying the night in a hostel in a place called Letterfrack. As I hung around in the communal living area drinking herbal tea with the other backpacking community, it was only a question of time before someone asked me the dreaded question.

'So what are you doing here in Ireland?'

In order to avoid a long, drawn-out conversation (the like of which I seemed to have engaged in hundreds of times already), I attempted to give as little away as possible. My caginess, however, only served to make everyone more inquisitive, and eventually I had to reveal that I was in Ireland because of a bet.

'Are you the guy with the fridge?' a girl asked, who up until now had been engrossed in her book.

'I am.'

She put her book down.

'You stole my lift.'

'What?'

'Yesterday. You stole my lift.'

Up until this moment, the coincidences in my life hadn't been that impressive. The best I had managed involved bumping into people I knew at airports. Sleeping in the same dormitory as the girl I had pushed in front of when hitching was probably going to edge into the lead. I owed her an apology.

'I'm so, so sorry,' I said.

'It's all right.'

'I would have asked the driver to stop for you too, but there simply wasn't room.'

'Because of the fridge, right?'

'Er, yes.'

'I waited two and a half hours there, you know.'

All right, don't make things worse. I felt bad enough as it was.

Tina was hitching around Ireland before returning to her native Denmark to study psychology. Like so many from her part of the world, she had that disarming ability to fully participate in an English conversation without anyone else needing to make the slightest compensation for the fact that it wasn't her native tongue. She was extremely pleasant and I began to feel very bad about the hitching business. Had we been in a hotel, I could have got to my feet and said that the least I could do was buy her a drink, perhaps even order a bottle of champagne, but in the present circumstances my hands were tied rather. All I could do was offer her a cup of someone else's lemon and ginger tea. In the event, I took her address in Denmark and promised to send her an atonement present.* She smiled courteously and went off to bed.

I had been forgiven, and I felt much better for it.

A great deal has been written and said about forgiveness. According to the Bible, Jesus was asked how many times you should forgive, and he said, 'Seventy times seven.' Everyone was quite confused for a while because at that time calculators hadn't been invented and arithmetic wasn't on the national curriculum. The general feeling, however, was that you should do it quite a lot.

'Forgive us our trespasses as we forgive those who trespass against us' is part of the Lord's Prayer that I was encouraged to say every day as part of assembly in school.

---

*As it happened, I eventually sent her a signed copy of *Round Ireland with a Fridge*. She must have been dead chuffed, because I never heard another word from her.

It's a pretty good message of all-round forgiveness. The trouble is, I don't see much evidence of forgiveness on show in present-day society. At the time of writing, Britain has the highest prison population per capita in Europe, and politicians seem to gain in popularity when their rhetoric endorses tougher sentencing for criminals. There doesn't seem to be much desire to reform or cure people, rather a hunger to see people punished.

When people become victims of a criminal act, they often instinctively respond by wanting revenge, and the problem with that is that it leads us into an escalation of the problem. By failing to offer forgiveness, those exacting the revenge make permanent enemies of those to whom they have meted out 'justice', and it may only be a matter of time before their enemies make them victims all over again.

Furthermore, the bearers of the grudge or carriers of resentment are weighed down by the negative thoughts that linger within them. This resentment is another form of anger. If we're angry we cannot be at peace. And if we're not at peace, then we won't be having peaceful thoughts and, consequently, if we accept that our thoughts and mood influence the events that unfold around us, then we won't be living in a very peaceful world.

Jesus was particularly good on what we should do with our enemies.

'Ye have heard that it hath been said,' he proclaimed, 'thou shalt love thy neighbour, and hate thine enemy; but I say unto you, love your enemies, bless them that curse you, do good to them that hate you …'

It would be nice, wouldn't it, if some of the world leaders who consider themselves to be good Christians might occasionally follow some of the teachings of their leader.

Forgiveness isn't always easy. For instance, how can I forgive someone if they've just been rude to me? Or told me a lie? Or been unfaithful to me? Or insisted that I watch an entire episode of *Big Brother*?

It helps if we are aware of why we are upset with someone in the first place. In very simple terms it is usually because they have behaved in a way that we didn't want them to. We didn't want them to be rude/tell us a lie/be unfaithful to us. But they did – and certainly nothing is going to change that.

We will find it easier to forgive properly if we can draw on two things, just as Tina was able to do.

Accept, and try to understand.

The hitch-hiker does both of these things, probably without realising. The hitcher, naturally enough, wants each car that comes by to stop and deliver him to his destination. However, the hitcher *accepts* that not every driver will do what he wants. He doesn't blame the driver of the car that doesn't stop. He doesn't shout angrily at every car that drives past him. No, because he *understands* that the driver of the car may have very good reasons why he doesn't want to stop. He may be in a hurry, too tired to talk, or he might not like the look of the hitcher, for whatever reason.

The hitcher accepts and understands this. However, it's not so easy to do this in everyday life. When someone behaves in a way that we don't want them to, we find it much harder to offer the kind of acceptance and understanding that the hitch-hiker offers to the driver who speeds past. We're more likely to be angry, hurt, or quick to blame.

The person who behaves badly towards us may be motivated by emotions that we don't much approve of – greed, anger, jealousy – but they will have their reasons for feeling the way they do. If we can accept that what has happened has happened (and how can we change that?), and get on with the job of trying to understand why the person might have behaved in such a way, then we reduce the amount of suffering we have to endure. It's like taking off a heavy rucksack. We're no longer carrying the burden of our own anger.

Accepting and understanding takes a lot of work, but ultimately we will be the beneficiaries. When people treat us without respect or fail comprehensively to deliver what we expect of them, perhaps we can take a lead from the hitch-hiker. We could observe that these people are simply like cars that aren't stopping for us, for whatever reason, and that we shouldn't allow them to drive us mad.

Let them drive by.

DRENCHED

It was mid-afternoon when I arrived at Matt Molloy's, and there were only six or seven customers in the pub. However, it wasn't long before the winning combination of fridge and rucksack had everyone discussing the merits and drawbacks of this kind of travel.

'How much was the bet for?' said Niamh, who was working behind the bar for the summer.

'A hundred pounds.'

'And how much was the fridge?' enquired an interested bystander called John.

'A hundred and thirty pounds.'

'Jeez, you're an eejit,' added Seamus, the pub manager.

'Niamh, get this man a pint,' concluded Geraldine, the boss and wife of the eponymous Matt, plus mother of Niamh.

I was beginning to understand how the Irish mentality worked. The more foolish, illogical or surreal one's actions were perceived to be (and mine surely fell into one of these categories), the wider the arms of hospitality were opened in salutation. I now found myself surrounded by inquisitive customers and staff. Brendan appeared from behind the bar where he had been stacking bottles.

'Has the fridge got a name?'

'Well, no, it hasn't.'

'Well, you've got to give the fridge a name. You can't be travelling round with a nameless fridge.'

A chorus of approval greeted Brendan's sentiments.

'What sex is it?' asked Etain.

Things were moving too fast for me.

'I hadn't given it much thought.'

'There must be a way of telling.'

Amid much amusement, a series of implausible methods were put forward, the most universally approved of which was proposed by John.

'What you have to do is you have to put it between two donkeys of either sex and see which one of the donkeys makes a move for the fridge.'

I was happy to accept this method as incontestable proof of the fridge's sex, but a distinct lack of donkeys restricted further progress down this particular scientific avenue.

'Why don't you give it a name which covers both sexes?' said Geraldine. 'You know, like Kim, Lesley or Val.'

'That's a good idea,' agreed Brendan, 'but you can't call a feckin' fridge Val!'

I concurred. No fridge of mine was going to be called Val.

'How about Saoirse?' suggested Seamus.

'Seersha?'

'Yes, Saoirse. It can be a boy or a girl's name, and it's Gaelic for "freedom". And you won't get many fridges experiencing more freedom than that one!' He had a point.

'Full name Saoirse Molloy,' said Geraldine.

'Sounds good to me,' I said, to cheers from the group. 'I hereby name this fridge Seersha Molloy.'

Geraldine was clearly moved by this new addition to the family, because she asked, 'Where are you staying, Tony?'

'Oh, I haven't sorted it yet. I was going to find a bed and breakfast.'

'You can stay in the flat above the pub if you want.'

'Really?'

'Niamh, go and get the keys. Let's put him and Saoirse upstairs for the night.'

'Are you sure? That's very kind.'

A good portion of my time on this trip was spent thanking people for their kindness.

I couldn't have expected that a brief mention of the fridge's surfing activity would cause such a furore. The response was immediate, and it was as if the gauntlet had been thrown down. My newfound friends took it upon themselves to rise to the challenge of coming up with something whacky for me and the fridge to do. The suggestion that Seamus should take it waterskiing was gaining in popularity, but Seamus, apparently a practical man, seemed to have some difficulty with this notion, although the rest of us couldn't see what the problem might be. Attach a rope, start the speedboat, and let Saoirse do the rest.

Geraldine introduced me to a couple called Tony and Nora, friends of her and Matt, who had been visiting for a long weekend.

'If you're ever down in Ennistymon, we'll take Saoirse scuba-diving,' said Tony, thrusting a piece of paper into my hand. 'Here's our address – you've no need to bother with hotels and the rest – you come and stay with us.'

'Are you sure that's not just the drink talking?' I joked.

'I don't drink,' he said, holding his orange juice proudly aloft.

This trip was full of surprises.

I t was early evening before I got a chance to look around Westport. It would have been shameful if all I had got to see of the place was the inside of Matt Molloy's pub. Westport had been a prosperous landlord town, designed by architect James Wyatt in the eighteenth century. It only took me ten minutes or so to do a full circuit and discover that its streets radiate from a focal point, the Octagon. There was a monument here with St Patrick on the top, proudly having taken the place of a British dignitary after the demise of British supremacy. The words beneath him made interesting reading:

> I AM PATRICK
> A SINNER MOST UNLEARNED
> THE LEAST OF ALL THE FAITHFUL
> AND UTTERLY DESPISED BY ALL

Now that guy had a self-esteem problem, no two ways about it.

I saw a signpost saying Westport Quay, and since it was a nice evening I decided to walk there. It turned out to be further than I had thought, but worth it. I was lucky enough now to be experiencing weather for which the west coast of Ireland is most definitely not renowned. Clear blue skies and a gently setting sun hung over Clew Bay as I headed up a dusty path towards a grand-looking house I had seen in the distance. It was quite magnificent, and in a wonderful location, with stunning views across the bay. It was clearly the landlord's home around which the entire town of Westport had been built, to house the estate workers. I climbed through a hole in the perimeter fence of the grounds and indulged in a little trespassing.* This was too special a house not to merit further investigation. Subsequently, I discovered that it was Westport House, and that by the following month it would be a commercialised tourist trap, but at the moment it was closed to the public and I genuinely believed I was getting a privileged glimpse of some palatial splendour that was off-limits to the hoi polloi.

On the walk back to Westport, out of nowhere some storm clouds appeared and the heavens opened. I tried to hitch back, but the irony was that, without the fridge, no one was remotely interested in stopping for me. For a few minutes I did everything I could to keep myself from getting soaked to the skin, but to no avail. It soon became apparent that a complete drenching was inevitable.

There was a definite moment when I surrendered to the rain: 'Okay, it's no use fighting this any more,' I said to myself, 'I'm just going to have to get wet.'

It was liberating and it felt good. I began to *enjoy* the rain. I could feel the moisture against my skin. It was cooling, somehow comforting. I raised my face to the sky, allowing the droplets to beat down on my skin. I smiled, knowing that I would soon be as wet as a man could be. What was the point of resisting? Why resist the irresistible? I was wet, and I might as well take pleasure in it. Provided that help wasn't too far away

---

* Forgive us our trespasses ...

and I could dry off again and change my clothes, this was nothing to fret about.

What I had experienced in that 'rain moment' was a kind of *positive surrender*. I had said to myself: 'I cannot change this, so I will accept it.' Then I went further – 'This is how it is. I will look for the positive in it' – and I actually began to take pleasure from what could have been seen as a negative experience.

If we can recognise the value of positive surrender, then we'll be more confident that we can deal with whatever comes along, and we'll find it much easier to stop trying to control events.

The hitch-hiker voluntarily relinquishes control the moment he or she begins the journey. Most of us, in our daily lives, fail to 'surrender to the roadside' in such an enlightened way. We spend so much time trying to be in control, in spite of the overwhelming evidence that we are *never* fully in control. Ever. Random events – train delays, blocked roads, terrorist alerts, freak weather conditions – are only a moment away from hijacking our carefully laid plans. When these 'events' happen, can we calmly take them in our stride and accept them as another 'adventure' – or will we be thrown into panic, experiencing a rush of emotions ranging from frustration to downright anger?

Life would be so much easier if we could learn just to do what we can, then leave it, saying to ourselves: 'This wasn't what I'd necessarily planned or anticipated, but it's happened now, so I may as well run with it. What else can I do?'

Acceptance of the way things are doesn't mean that we become the victims of events. Nor does it mean that we simply take everything that comes our way without defending our position or standing up for what we believe is right. What it does mean, however, is that we recognise the difference between things over which we can have some influence, and those we cannot.

Some of us try to control everything in our lives. Some of us make rigid plans for the future. Nothing wrong with plans, provided they're not too specific and instead represent more of a general direction for us to head in. However, sometimes these game plans become quite specific. We probably all know someone who has said they are going to make a million by the time they're forty. Or to have had three kids by the time they're thirty-five. Or to have made that promotion by the end of the year. Or to have that fast car within five years ...

We over-complicate things by being too specific about what we want and when we want it. And besides, what makes us so sure that we *know* what's best for us anyway? We only have to think back to some of the desires we held when we were children, teenagers and young adults to see how much we change in our ideas of what we want. Don't we find it slightly embarrassing now when we think about the clothes we wanted to wear, the person we wanted to date, the car we wanted to drive and the people we wanted to impress? When I was eight I wanted to be a vet. When I was sixteen I wanted to be a pop star. When I was thirty I wanted to marry someone and live happy ever after. When I was forty I wanted to be sixteen. None of those things happened. Other things happened instead, that were equally good, if not better.

The fridge-hiker knows best.

Allow things to unfold. *

---

* Deckchairs in particular.

Jigs, Reels and Songs from the Heart

The nation needed an update on my recent adventures. On air, Gerry Ryan astutely picked up on one common thread that ran through them all.

'Tony, you seem to be spending most of your time in pubs. I think it's important to point that out at this stage.'

'Well, the trouble is, Gerry, I can't get out of them. I go in and I've got a fridge in tow and it isn't long before the exit door is barred and that's it, I'm stuck there.'

'I must use that as an excuse myself one day.'

He was right, of course; I had been spending most of my time in pubs. The irony is that the one night when I didn't go anywhere near one, I ended up with less than two hours' sleep.

'Watch out for him, folks,' said Gerry, winding up our interview. 'He's heading for Ennistymon today, so if you see a gentleman looking reasonably benign with a fridge by his side, please do stop and say hello, and if he doesn't seem threatening, well, then, please give him a lift. Bon voyage once again, Tony – we'll keep in touch.'

I pulled the fridge down to the roadside, tired from the excesses of the journey, but knowing that these conversations I had on national radio were the equivalent of filling a vehicle's petrol tank. I was fresh in the minds of the nation's drivers, and once they set eyes on the fridge, they were only too happy to throw open that passenger door.

I was on my way to Ennistymon because I had a friend to meet there – Tony, the teetotaller who had offered to take the fridge scuba-diving.

The hitch went well, as ever, and Paddy, a greenkeeper at the local golf course, was my final ride of the day. When he stopped, he had thought I had bought the fridge in town and was bringing it home. It was reassuring to get lifts from people who weren't aware of what I was doing as a result of hearing it on the radio. It proved that the task in hand could be achieved without media assistance, though it was questionable whether it would be as much fun. From the car I called Tony and arranged to meet him at a pub called Daly's in Ennistymon's main street.

In Ennistymon I felt like I was in the unspoiled heart of rural Ireland. It was a pretty place with colourful shop fronts and an abundance of small bars, but there was no sense of all this being there for the benefit of tourists. I looked up and down the main street and counted more than twenty bars. Presently I learned that at one time there had been forty-two, all there largely to serve the customers for the cattle market, which used to swell the town's population many times over.

I located Daly's, a tiny bar directly next to two others – Davoren's and P. Begley's. I noted that P. Begley's was closed and assumed it had fallen victim to the intense competition. I walked into Daly's and was greeted by the usual turning of surprised heads. One head wasn't so surprised. Tony's.

'Ah look! The eejit has landed!' he announced.

A pint was poured and the fridge was lifted to a place of honour on a bar stool alongside us, and to any pub newcomer it would have appeared like just another regular drinker. Tony told me he had to go and pick up his daughter from school and that when he got back he'd take me on a sightseeing tour of the area.

I noticed that a man with a healthy head of white hair and matching beard had been surveying the fridge with interest as he slowly supped on his pint. After a few minutes we made eye contact, and he nodded to me, pointing at the fridge on its bar stool.

'Ah sure, it's nice enough to see it out of context.'

I was delighted by the measured delicacy of his remark and I went and joined him and spent a delightful hour in his company until Tony returned to take me on his sightseeing excursion.

The tour included the dramatic Cliffs of Moher, the village of Doolin, Lisdoonvarna and the Burren smoke-house, where Tony's sister-in-law worked. She was a bubbly woman who insisted on showing me a video usually shown to tourists of how a salmon is smoked. I patiently sat through it despite having no interest in it whatsoever (I had never considered being au fait with the procedure involved in smoking a salmon a social advantage), and afterwards I was rewarded with a good-sized portion of the final product to take away. The irony was that I had no way of keeping it fresh, even though I was touring the country with a fridge.

Apart from the woman who was serving behind the bar, the evening clientele of Cooley's were entirely male, and I was the youngest by some margin. There was a chap playing the banjo rather well up at the far end of the bar, and a less competent guitarist attempting to accompany him. As Tony and I walked in, the resident drunk called out, 'Hey, Tony, go and get your box.'

At first I thought it was someone calling for me to go and get my fridge, but the other Tony disappeared outside and made for his car. I smiled to those present, keen to give the impression that I knew what a 'box' was, and why one might be needed on a social occasion like this. The drunk, doing his utmost to focus his bloodshot eyes on me, put his hand on my shoulder in a gesture of friendship which serendipitously also prevented him from falling over. He explained need-lessly, 'He's gone to get his box.'

Yes, I thought, and there was a good chance we would be putting this fellow in it at the end of the evening.

Tony returned with an accordion, and musicians and instruments materialised from nowhere. The resident drunk produced a pair of spoons from his pocket and proceeded to play them with great skill and dexterity. After the ability to order a drink, this must have been the last of his faculties to go. I had always thought of the spoons as being played as a novelty purely to get laughs, but in the correct hands it made an authentic percussive instrument. The four-piece band became a five-piece when Willy Daly entered carrying a bodhrán (the tambouriney drum hit with a double-ended stick) and joined the merry band of players. He must have had a device within him that could sound out when a session was beginning.

What followed was a great treat for me. This was Irish traditional music as I had hoped to see and hear it, spontaneous and from the heart, and not produced for the sake of the tourist industry. As I sat there with my pint in my hand, enjoying the jigs and the reels, I watched the joy in the faces of the players and of those

around them, who tapped their feet and applauded enthusiastically. Music the joybringer. No question of being paid, or any requirement to perform for a certain amount of time. Just play for as long as it makes you feel good. This was self-expression, not performance. Someone would begin playing a tune and the fellow musicians would listen to it once through, hear how it went and join in when they felt comfortable, until, on its last run-through, it was being played with gusto by the entire ensemble. This process provided each piece with the dynamic of a natural crescendo that could almost have been orchestrated.

The banjo player was from out of town, but his playing assured him the hospitality that might be showered on a long-lost son. He had an extremely large belly hanging over his trousers, which were held up by a belt that looked incapable of withstanding the strain. Were it to break, then his weight would be redistributed to such a degree that he would surely topple forwards. It was too much responsibility for a belt that was showing signs of fraying.

He bonded with Tony, recognising him for the accomplished accordion player he was, and they smiled at each other in mutual admiration. The less talented guitarist continued to play, providing the right and wrong chords in equal measure. Though at times he spoiled the sound the combo was producing, he received no admonishment or looks of censure, and was made as welcome as the most able musician.

After an hour or so, the unaccompanied singing began. For this, each singer would close their eyes and present their party piece to a reverent audience, who would offer their comments on the lyrics at the end of each song. Songs were sung in turn, much in the same way that drinkers in an English pub might exchange jokes. Some patiently waited, anxious to display their talents, and others had to have a song coaxed out of them. Significantly, the ones who had to be encouraged gave the best performances, but there was no competitive element, and each singer, good or bad, was given commensurate respect. I racked my brains for a song I could sing should I be asked, but happily the honour wasn't bestowed upon me. I made a mental note to come up with something for these occasions, because I liked this approach to singing – closing your eyes and belting it out from the heart. It seemed like a style tailor-made for the drunk, but Tony proved that intoxication wasn't essential, as his contribution, the product of four soft drinks, was one of the most heartfelt and soulful renditions of the evening.

I now realise that what had been amazing about this evening was that there'd been a definite feeling that no one had performed better than anyone else. I'm not sure that I've felt that before or since, when I've been in a place where people have been singing and playing.

Imagine if the people in that room had told the less talented guitarist to stop playing because he was getting some of the chords wrong. Yes, the overall sound would have been more musical – but would the overall atmosphere have been as good? Sometimes, it seems, we benefit by putting up with stuff.

Tolerate, and try not to judge.

The fridge-hiker certainly has to.

When I get a lift, I have to listen to the view of my driver, even if it happens to be poles apart from the view that I hold. I have respect for the driver, not because I agree with him, but because he has had the good grace to allow me into his car and help me on my way. The driver may hold any number of obnoxious views abhorrent to me – but what is there to be gained by locking horns and arguing with him? It may end up spoiling my morning – and do I have time for that? No, I don't.

It seems to me that my time is better spent by converting a negative thought about somebody into a positive one. I benefit more by focusing on the driver's good points – like the fact that he was kind enough to offer me a lift – and by trying to find some common ground where we can engage in a pleasant exchange. I may offer up a gentle rebuff to one of his bigoted views, but I'll do it in a lighthearted way, not with the intention of proving that *I'm right and he's wrong*. The main thing is that we're on a journey together and we need to get somewhere.

Much earlier in my trip I learned something valuable from the good people in a pub in Sligo as we'd all tried to watch the FA Cup Final on the TV.

The pub was large and it looked like three separate rooms had all been knocked through to create an open-plan effect. Two large screens at each end provided the focus for everyone's attention. Everyone, that is, except for the most drunk man in Ireland, who had confetti in his hair and a smartish suit, suggesting that he had come straight from a wedding reception. Presumably he had drunk the free bar dry, and his hand had been forced into carrying on his good work elsewhere. Using his tie as a microphone he stood at one end of the pub, just below the TV screen, and sang his interpretation of the Boomtown Rats' 'I Don't Like Mondays'. It was tuneless and loud. Too close to the original for my taste. He then began jumping around as if someone had put five thousand volts through his body. If it hadn't been for his exclamation, none of us in that pub would have had the faintest idea what he was doing.

'EAT YOUR HEART OUT, MICHAEL FLATLEY!!' he bellowed at the top of his voice.

Ah, that was it then. He was doing *River Dance*. His exertions were such that I thought he was going to have a heart attack there and then. Instead he tipped up his pint mug and shared some of the beer within it between his mouth and his suit.

This man was creating an enormous distraction for the majority of those in the pub who, like me, were there primarily to watch a game of football. But there wasn't a sign of any antagonism towards him. The drinkers simply smiled, laughed or shook their heads good-humouredly. This hadn't been my natural reaction, but I soon realised that the best way to diffuse my irritation was to smile along with the rest. If you can't beat them or join them, laugh at them. You'll have a much better day.

'KEEP AN EYE ON THAT FRIDGE OF YOURS'

Reaching Listowel in County Kerry, having crossed the Shannon by ferry, I allowed myself a celebratory drink in a bar, given that I figured I was more than halfway round Ireland by now. Following the usual commotion that resulted once the fridge had been identified, I was approached by two scruffy-looking fellows, both in overalls covered in muck.

'Are you a bachelor?' one of them asked.

'Yes, I am,' I replied, a little suspiciously.

'Course he is,' said the other. 'You don't think a wife would let him take off round Ireland with a feckin' fridge in tow, would you?'

'Why do you want to know?' I enquired, defensively.

'Well, there's a bachelor festival in Ballyduff tonight, and we were just talking and saying how it might be a laugh if you entered. You could enter the fridge too, unless the feckin' thing is married.'

I had no idea, really. I assumed that when you buy a fridge brand-new, it's single. That's the danger of buying a reconditioned number; you've no idea how many acrimonious divorces it may have been through.

'Maybe it's married to him,' said the one with the moustache.

'They're travelling together, aren't they? Maybe they're on their honeymoon.'

The pub clientele were in fits of laughter. It was time to set the record straight.

'The fridge and I aren't married. We are just good friends and there's nothing going on between us.'

I was in the company of Brian and Joe, who laid hard-wood floors for a living, and who both knew the owner of the bar where this bachelor festival was taking place. I was urged by the rest of the drinkers in the pub to take them up on their offer, and soon I was in the back of their van heading towards Ballyduff, and yet another bizarre evening.

Bachelor festivals, or this one at any rate, turned out to entail little more than a succession of single men spending a small amount of time on stage doing some kind of unimpressive party piece while a drunken rabble looked on. In spite of my experience as a performer, I floundered around on stage as much as any of the other 'bachelors', unable to recall any material that might have been suitable for the crowd before me, who weren't far off resembling a baying mob. I was close to doing what comedians commonly call 'dying on your arse'. Brian saved the day, as it happened. Just as the crowd's heckling was about to turn to boos, he marched up the middle of the dance floor with my fridge and deposited it next to me.

'It's the fridge! It's the fridge!' shouted more than a few excited punters.

'Hey, look how good they are together!' someone yelled. 'I reckon he's not a bachelor after all!'

'I am!' I protested. 'But we're part of a team. It's a case of "Love me, love my fridge."'

For some reason, this drew a huge cheer from the audience and I was able to exit shortly afterwards with my fragile dignity intact.

Soon afterwards I noted that the fridge was up one end of the dance floor, completely surrounded by young women anxious to sign it with pens, crayons and whatever else they could lay their hands on. Myself and the other bachelors who had taken part looked on, rather dismayed.

'I'd keep an eye on that fridge of yours,' said one of the bachelors. 'Someone will try to nick that, I reckon.'

'I doubt it,' I said.

'Sure they will – after all, it's a fridge celebrity now. Someone will have their eye on it. Will I go and rescue it for you?'

'No, leave it. The people are having fun.'

By this time I was immune to such a concern. I knew that if anyone stole my fridge it wouldn't be a bad thing anyway. For starters, it would just make for a funny chapter in the book that I was planning to write, and besides, as I pointed out to these people, if my fridge was stolen, then I could always get another one.

'Ah,' people would say, 'but it wouldn't be the same, though, would it?'

'No. It would be a different fridge. But my journey would be the same.'

A shrug usually followed such a remark. Sometimes the simpler the message, the harder it is to understand.

It was at this point that I really did begin to consider the nature of possessions. I'd already acquired the wisdom from the King of Tory – *we need less than we think we do* – but it occurred to me that possessions can still cause us problems, even if we have very few. Even if we have just one possession, as I pretty much did on this trip – my fridge – and we begin to treasure that possession and to see it as 'vital' to us, then we are putting our happiness in danger.

Being relaxed about whether my fridge was stolen was surprising to people.

'But it's a special fridge!' they would say.

Perhaps it was special. But *we* had created its 'specialness' – me and Ireland together. If we had done it once with one fridge, then why couldn't we do it again with another? After all, hadn't it been the case that it was in the *process* of creating the specialness that we had found the joy? The fridge itself wasn't the source of the happiness. A symbol, maybe, of that joy, but not the source. It was nice to have it, sure it was, but why waste energy and worry on trying to hang on to it?

The weird thing is that the fridge didn't really feel like it *belonged* to me. Part of the joy of it was that it seemed to *belong* to everybody. Certainly nobody bothered to ask my permission before scrawling a message of goodwill on to it in marker pen. By the end of the night of the bachelor festival, there was no more space left on it for new messages. People treated this fridge as if it was their own – although I noted that they stopped short of putting beers in it. I began to recognise that I was little more than the custodian of the fridge.

This attitude towards ownership has more in common with cultures that are often looked down on by the West. For example, the Australian Aborigines have never believed that they *own* the land, rather that they are custodians of it. They see the landscape more as a *companion*, for want of a better word, so the idea of chopping it up, fencing it and owning it has always been alien to them. There is no individual ownership.

This is a very interesting way of approaching life. Yes, having no individual ownership may not work in today's society, but it worked for the Aborigines for tens of thousands of years – until the Europeans came along and messed it all up for them. Nowadays, I look at the things around me and try to view myself as their custodian, rather than their owner. I have them, and I can enjoy having them – but I don't *have* to have a good many of them, and if events take them from me, then I don't have to become distressed.

I didn't need to worry about losing my fridge. By looking beneath the surface we can see that the fridge was merely a catalyst enabling people to recognise the joy that was available to them every day of their lives – provided they knew how to tap into it. I didn't *want* to lose my fridge, but if it happened, I was ready to deal with it without suffering.

Be prepared for loss.

We could ask the big question: does anybody really own anything anyway? Ownership isn't a natural law. It's man-made. The ownership of most land can be traced back to a time when someone stuck a stake in the ground and said, 'This is mine because I got here first.' (Sometimes having killed someone who was already there or who looked like they were going to get there before them.) Without laws and police forces to back us up, then many of the things we call 'ours' could just as easily be somebody else's.

By thinking of myself as a trustee rather than an owner, I make less of an attachment to the 'thing' I own, and I suffer less if and when I lose it. After all, what's the point of suffering over the loss of something when we're going to lose everything in the end anyway?

Well, *aren't we*? No one, as far as I know, has cracked immortality yet.

FRIDGE POWER

In Cork I looked with some satisfaction at the considerable traffic and substantial buildings around me. It had been some time since I had been anywhere with this much vitality. Although it didn't strike me as being a particularly beautiful city, nonetheless I had a good feeling about it. I was just considering my next course of action when I was approached by a middle-aged Scot.

'You must be Tony, and that must be your fridge,' he said, forthrightly.

'It is and I am. I mean, I am and it is.'

I was making no sense, but he didn't mind. He had been following my progress on the radio and kept insisting how wonderful an idea it had been to travel with a fridge. Then, two minutes into our acquaintance, came the offer.

'If you've no sorted anywhere to stay, ye can come and stop with me and me wife Sheila. We'll sort ye out, give ye a chance to clean up, do your washing and all the rest of it.'

'That's very kind … er …'

'Dave. The name's Dave Stewart.'

'Thanks, Dave. It's just that I haven't made any plans just yet. I thought I might head to a pub called Westimers.'

'Oh aye. Do you know someone there?'

'Not really, it's just that on the first morning I spoke to Gerry Ryan, they called in and said if I ever came to Cork, they'd throw a fridge party for me.'

'Oh aye. I heard that. Good idea.'

Dave gave me directions to Westimers and wrote out his address and phone number should I want to take him up on his kind offer. I crossed the road and a student came rushing out from inside a pub demanding to sign the fridge. I was still very much in the world of the splendidly off-kilter, and I liked it.

At Westimers there was much surprise that I had responded to an offer made nearly three weeks previously.

'Eric will be sick that he's missed you,' said Alan the barman.

Eric, the boss and original instigator of the offer of the fridge party, was away on a fishing trip in County Mayo and couldn't be contacted. Still, no matter, that was no reason for the rest of the staff not to make a fuss of me, and I was given drinks and the now standard free lunch. The decor of the pub explained its rather odd name, Westimers. The Wild West was its theme and the walls were adorned with saddles, stetsons and gun-wielding cowboys. Perhaps it was his love of the American West that had originally caused Eric to take *my* pioneering quest to heart.

I had just begun talking with a lunching businessman at the bar about how I was considering making a trip down to Kinsale when Alan interrupted, 'Tony, there's a phone call for you.'

This was weird. No one knew I was here. Correction: one person did.

'Hello, Tony, it's Dave here. You know, Dave you just met on the pavement. Now stay where you are, I've been on to my mate who is the features editor at the *Evening Echo*. Don't go anywhere because they're sending a reporter down to meet you.' Things moved fast in Cork.

One newspaper interview later, I returned to my pint and was soon approached by a young man called Barry who told me he could take me to Kinsale in a quarter of an hour. Things moved very fast in Cork.

Everyone in Westimers thought it was a good idea if I used Cork as a base for a few days' sightseeing, not least because that meant if Eric phoned they could tell him of my arrival and see if he wanted to go ahead with the fridge party. There was much amusement among the staff as they watched me pack my fridge as an overnight bag, a role that hadn't been asked of it since my jaunt to Tory Island.

Okay, the quarter of an hour was closer to an hour, but just as he had said he would, Barry was soon transporting me to my next destination. It was somehow in keeping with my trip that he should turn out to be a sales rep for Caffrey's, and that his first call at the Hole In The Wall pub in Kinsale necessitated my drinking complimentary pints while he went about his business. The fridge and beer had developed a truly symbiotic relationship, and together they were unstoppable. Things happened.

A canvassing Labour politician marched past the pub garden with his entourage, and spotted me and the fridge holding court with a number of intrigued fellow drinkers. He obviously felt that the notoriety this fridge had gained in his country meant that being photographed alongside it could enhance his chances of election. His aides hastily organised a photoshoot, and suddenly there was Michael Calnan with his arm round me, beaming unnaturally and toasting the fridge with a pint of Caffrey's, supplied by the equally opportunistic

Barry. Kieran, the owner of the pub, was just attempting to usher all of us round to the left so that the name of his pub formed the backdrop, when Barry noticed that a traffic warden was putting a parking ticket on his car. There then followed an extraordinary scene in which Barry attempted to get the ticket rescinded, for which he produced in his defence a Labour politician and a man pulling a fridge behind him. Against such formidable opposition, the meter maid put up a sterling effort at insisting that the ticket should stand, but when the chorus of drinkers in the pub garden chimed in with a chant of 'Let him off, let him off, he's driving the man with the fridge!' she finally capitulated. There was no doubting that the politician had borne little influence, and that it had been the fridge which had swayed things. You've heard of 'People Power'? Well, now please welcome 'Fridge Power'. Already it had got someone off a parking ticket – there was no knowing what merito-rious cause of downtrodden citizen against oppressive state it would embrace next.

When the fridge and I returned from our political struggle, we learned that Kieran hadn't been idle. He had organised a boat trip for the next morning round Kinsale's harbour, and complimentary accommodation at the White House Hotel opposite. Barry then went about arranging me a free bar meal with another Caffrey's customer, a restaurant around the corner called the Blue Haven.

Honestly, what a day! I hadn't been able to put a foot wrong since I'd arrived in Ireland's second city. It was as if a spell had been cast in which I could have anything I wanted. It was just a shame the magic had worn off by the time I made my clumsy and slurred advances towards Brenda, the Blue Haven's waitress. Her haven, whatever colour it was, remained firmly off-limits.

In the morning, Pat Collins's little fishing boat did us proud. I wondered what Kieran had said to Pat the previous night, because he quite happily gave up an hour and a half of his morning and entirely without ulterior motive took a man and his fridge on a tour of the harbour, indicating any points of interest. He helped me on and off the boat with the fridge, and even posed for a photograph with his arm round it, but saw no reason in wasting any time enquiring as to what the hell I was doing with the bloody thing. I suppose he felt that those were questions for a younger man to ask.

From the helm Pat turned round and gestured behind us: 'You want to watch that fridge,' he said.

I smiled, delighted by Pat's concern and the gentle absurdity of his words. '*You want to watch that fridge.*' It was almost as if the fridge had a reputation for profligacy and philandering. God forbid. It hadn't even been plugged in.

I f I'd needed proof that having 'faith in the fridge' worked, and that the basic tenets of the fridge-hiking philosophy were sound, then the previous twenty-four hours had delivered it to me. Since arriving in Cork I had been carried on a wave of goodwill, and I'd not even been allowed to put my hand in my pocket to pay for a single thing. For the moment at least, the Fridge Man was the honorary guest of the Irish people, who somehow instinctively embraced his naive, harmless and downright silly quest.

Pat Collins had told me to *watch that fridge*. I would follow his advice, and in watching it I would observe the wisdom that emerged in its wake.

The fridge-hiker does a lot of *watching*. The fridge-hiker observes the day, and each event that unfolds, almost with an objective eye – partly because the fridge journey itself is an event, a stunt of sorts. Once I had decided that the unfolding story was going to be worth writing about, I began to observe all the more, and I began to realise that this was helping me to be *in* every moment.

Many activities require us to be in the moment. On this journey I noted that driving happens to be one of them. As I sat in the passenger seat of the many cars that carried me through the country, I observed that the drivers didn't spend much time looking in the mirror at the road behind them. Nor did they concern themselves too greatly with the road that was a long way ahead. Most of the time they were watching the road directly in front of them. They did this naturally, knowing this to be the best way to preserve their own safety and wellbeing. When they did look in the mirror at what was behind them, they did it only to see if someone was about to overtake, and when they looked a long way ahead it was to ensure they weren't going to drive headlong into a pile-up.

What can the fridge-hiker learn from this?

Drivers know that if they spend too much time looking too far ahead or directly behind them, then they are more likely to have an accident. So, if we spend too long thinking about the past (thoughts that may often be tinged with regret, guilt or bitterness) – or too long thinking about the future (thoughts that might be dominated by fear, desire or expectation), then we're not able to give our proper attention to what's happening *right now*. And *right now* is all we have. It's the old adage that I always used to hear as a kid.

Tomorrow never comes.

A SPLINTER

By the time I got to Wexford I'd been on the road for nearly three weeks. I'd been in pubs for most of those evenings and I'd seen many attractive women along the way. In Cork I'd shared a drunken kiss with an art student called Mary, but I'd managed to fall off the wall on which we'd both been perched and for some reason the liaison had failed to develop. (Many women wrongly take falling off a wall as a sign of incompetence.)

I checked into a hostel run by a fun guy called Butch, who happened to have a pretty girl from New Zealand working for him. Karen was helping out with odd jobs at the hostel before resuming her travels. She came in carrying a dustpan and brush and sat down to join me and Butch for tea.

'I've finished for the day. Thank goodness for that,' she said.

The subject turned inevitably to fridge travel and I found that now I could almost answer every question by rote. I got off the subject by firing questions at Karen about her travels, questions with which she must have been equally familiar.

'Do people just assume you're Australian at first?' I asked.

'Yeah. But the accent is different, you know.'

'Yes. Don't you say *sex* instead of *six*?'

'Apparently. Australians are always trying to get us to say it. They ask questions like "What's eight minus two?" But we're wise to it and we just answer, "Half a dozen."'

I found myself contemplating what 'half a dozen' with her might be like.

'I like your red shorts,' said Karen. 'They're cool.'

'Thanks.'

I was unable to return the compliment with a flattering remark about what I had just been admiring about her. It wouldn't have been considered good manners.

I slept badly that night. Not surprising, given that I was sharing a room with four lads from Dublin who were down in Wexford with the seeming intention of drinking as much as they could and then filling their dorm with as many noxious gases as was humanly possible.

'I'm not sleeping in there for another night,' I said. 'My body simply won't take it.'

'I think you're going to have to,' said Karen. 'Everywhere in Wexford is full for the next two nights, and you'll find it the same all the way up the coast between here and Dublin.'

'Well I'm not going back in that room except to get my stuff out,' I protested. 'That room is the smelliest room on earth. It's frightening to think that only four arses could produce such a putrefying stench.'

'Just another one of the many miracles of the human body,' said Butch flippantly, who proceeded to point to the corner of the garden. 'You could always sleep in the doghouse.'

Everyone laughed. Except me. I looked. The doghouse. The doghouse, eh? I got to my feet and wandered over to have a closer look at it. It was a small wooden structure about six feet long, and four feet high at the apex of its pitched roof. I looked inside and saw that it was full of junk.

'Where's the dog?' I enquired.

'That went with the girlfriend, but the doghouse stayed. It's a kind of shrine to the failure of our relationship,' said Butch.

Never mind shrine, it was an oasis! In present circumstances, a very appealing piece of real estate. I got down on my hands and knees and crawled in a little way. It was dark and had a musty smell, but compared to a room occupied by a quartet of farters, this was a herb garden.

'Tony, get out of there, it's full of bricks and building shite,' said Butch.

'Yes, but I could clear that out.'

'Don't be stupid, man, it's a doghouse. You're not seriously thinking of sleeping in it?'

'I am. It's got everything. A secluded location, privacy and an ensuite toilet,' I said, pointing to the garden.

My earnestness was greeted with incredulity. Butch and Karen couldn't see what I could clearly see – that sleeping in the doghouse was vastly preferable to what was on offer in my present room. Above all, it meant I could get an early night and allow sleep the healer to repair some of the mental and physical damage of the past three weeks. Without it I could collapse.

'I bet you wouldn't sleep in there,' said Karen.

'Careful,' said Butch. 'He's a dangerous man to bet with. I mean, look what he's doing with that fridge.'

'He's too tall to fit in it. He won't do it,' reiterated Karen.

'I bet I do. I bet you a hundred pounds I do.'

'I haven't got a hundred pounds.'

'You will have in the morning,' interjected a very amused Butch.

'All right, then: sixteen pence. I bet you sixteen pence I sleep in this doghouse tonight,' I said, proffering my hand for the sealing handshake.

'Okay. Sixteen pence it is.'

Karen took my hand in hers and we shook. It was a long, lingering handshake; in fact, it just seemed to keep on going. Karen made no attempt to release my hand, and for some reason I felt that the onus was on her to do the releasing. As we shook, we looked into each other's eyes, a moment that was almost embarrassing in its intimacy. In the corner of my eye, I was aware of Butch nervously shuffling in his seat. I gulped. I must learn to stop doing that. I don't think it's particularly cool.

It was me who released the handshake. I had become unnerved by the eye thing. Some different form of communication had just gone on, and although the meaning seemed clear enough, history had shown that this was a language I was well capable of misinterpreting. Karen, I suspected, spoke the language fluently. Most girls do. Boys don't speak it at all, but just understand a smattering of key words. Their job is not to make a pig's ear of the translation. They normally fail quite spectacularly.

It took an hour and a half to clear out the 'building shite', as Butch had so eloquently described it. On completion I surveyed the new sleeping quarters. Spartan, yes, a little bleak maybe, but they were dry, and the weather looked set on remaining glorious, so the suspect roof was an irrelevance. All in all it was accommodation fit for a king – of Tory, anyway.

That night, in spite of being exhausted from the excesses of this adventure, I took Karen to the pub for a drink, where we continued to get on particularly well.

'Would you like to come back to my place for a coffee?' I said when we got back to the hostel.

Karen laughed.

'Are you *really* going to sleep in there?'

'Sixteen pence is sixteen pence. I'd be a fool not to. Why don't you join me in there for a nightcap?'

'Okay.' She giggled.

I was in new territory. I had never invited a girl back to a doghouse before.

We made two coffees in the kitchen, carried them out to the garden and climbed into my lodgings.

'Hey, it's surprisingly cosy,' said Karen.

And it was too. Before leaving for the pub, I had filled it with cushions taken from the living room, and unzipped my sleeping bag and laid it out like a bed cover.

'What you need in here are some candles,' remarked Karen.

'Yes, I haven't got the lighting quite right.'

It was pitch darkness.

'I'll go and get some,' she said keenly.

For someone with 16p at stake, she was acting quite irresponsibly.

The candles almost completed the transition of doghouse to love nest. The rest was up to me. Karen was showing all the signs of someone who wasn't going to slap my face if I leant over to kiss her. I decided to have a go. I took a deep breath and attempted to swivel round so I was facing her, but cracked my head on the low part of the pitched roof. Not unnaturally, it hurt quite a lot, but I made a snap decision to try to complete the kiss regardless. It was made difficult by the fact that Karen had begun laughing uncontrollably. I stopped short of her mouth, and suddenly saw the funny side myself, breaking into fits of giggles. The moment of passion had been hijacked by hilarity. I hoped this wasn't going to be a feature of all my future lovemaking.

The laughter subsided. There we were, inches apart, directly under the apex of the roof, so with ample head-room. Surely now the kiss was inevitable. Slowly I moved my mouth towards hers. She closed her eyes, I closed mine and we waited for my gentle forward momentum to bring us together. Until a voice outside halted it.

'Are you guys really in there?'

Butch, clearly back from the pub, had arrived.

'Make way for me, I'm coming in,' he shouted.

I hoped the neighbours weren't hearing all this.

Butch was impressively drunk. He treated his reluctant audience to an embittered diatribe, the main theme of which was the present unsatisfactory state of his love life. It was very funny, and even in these circumstances he had us both laughing. But funny or not, we still wanted him to go. He seemed blissfully unaware that his tirade about unsatisfactory sexual liaisons was preventing the initiation of a new one.

'Oscar Wilde summed it all up,' he railed. '"What is love? It is when two fools misunderstand each other."'

I thought yes, and will you please bugger off and give the two of us a chance to misunderstand each other. We've been dying to misunderstand each other for the past hour and a half. In fact, the only thing we have been able to understand about each other is that we're desperate to do a bit of misunderstanding. *Understand?*

Eventually he left, but not before wheeling the fridge up to the door, saying, 'I've brought the fridge along to keep an eye on you both.'

Yes, yes. Very funny. Now GO!

There is a reason why people don't make love in doghouses more often. Dogs don't even do it. They would rather suffer the indignity of doing it outside with people watching than do it in a doghouse. To our credit though, Karen and I had a go, and under the circumstances I think we did pretty well. One of the main problems was that the doghouse was too short for my body, and my feet had to stick out of the door. With this particular evening being a clear and chilly one, this meant I had cold feet throughout the entire proceedings, in more ways than one. Because of this need for exterior feet dangling, the doghouse had to be left open, and this allowed occasional gusts of cool breeze to penetrate areas where one wouldn't normally welcome a rush of cold air. The lack of headroom also proved problematical on occasions, and if either of us lost concentration or momentarily forgot where we were (difficult, but hey, I like to think it could happen), then we were all too quickly reminded of our immediate vicinity with a blow to the head.

All in all, the artificial obstacles we had to overcome made the whole encounter feel like an event in *It's a Knockout*. (The mini marathon, I like to think.) We had

represented Banbury as best we could, but it was unlikely that our performance had been enough to nudge us ahead of Kettering and on to further competition in Europe.

I woke in the morning and looked outside. There was the fridge looking back at me. It was jealous, no doubt about it, but that was understandable enough. After all, it had never been plugged in, and now I had.

And I had a splinter to prove it.

When I sat down to write *Round Ireland with a Fridge* once the whole adventure was over, I didn't want to include this 'doghouse episode' in the book. I wasn't sure that it showed me in a good light – I mean, how immature had I been? Shouldn't I have known better at my age?

In the end I decided that if I was going to write a book that did justice to this amazing journey I'd just had (and that was my intention), then I should simply recount the facts as entertainingly as I could, and not concern myself with what people might think of me.

And so I told the truth. I figured that what happened was funny, and in keeping with the whole ridiculous affair, so I just told it how it was. After *Round Ireland with a Fridge* was published I was expecting to receive a certain amount of flak or criticism from people about my behaviour – particularly with regard to the doghouse chapter. I was surprised, however, to discover that no one seemed particularly bothered, and that the people who mentioned it weren't judgmental. It was almost as if they accepted me for how I was and ran with it. My fears had painted an entirely different picture from the one that reality eventually delivered.

I'm glad, then, that I told it how it was. It's quite a temptation for all of us to make subtle 'rewrites' of events that have taken place in our lives. Sometimes, if we repeat the 'rewrite' enough, we can even begin to forget the real events that actually took place. Sometimes we'll create the 'rewrite' because we want to be right. On other occasions it will be because we don't want to disappoint somebody, and sometimes because we want someone to think of us in a better light.

Whatever the reason, what we don't necessarily realise is that ultimately we are actually hurting ourselves. Deep down, *we know the truth*. Although we may not admit it to others, or even ourselves, at our deepest core we know what the truth is. As a result of our denial of this truth, we'll be carrying a burden of guilt, whether we know it or not, which will inhibit the growth of our own self-esteem.

If you're reading this book and only spotting things within it that may refer to *other people* (e.g. 'That's Alison – she's always worrying,' or 'That's so true of Mark – he's always judging people'), then try to look at it again but this time specifically focusing on yourself. Be brutally honest but do it in a positive way, knowing that there is nothing wrong with *not being perfect*. Nobody is perfect, except deep down in the part of us that we've forgotten about, the very core of our souls, where we may be pretty damn close to it. On the exterior, this is where we display all our fears, and they manifest themselves in jealousy, meanness, lack of tolerance, playing the victim, the attribution of blame, aggression, anger, indecision or self-aggrandisement. So:

Be honest with yourself.

Never mind that you may not have always been an angel. Who has? You don't need to deny the things that you think might have been your failings. Don't make yourself feel guilty about them. After all, the person who has really suffered the most from your actions is none other than *you*. What goes around comes around.

If you find yourself troubled by some of your actions of the past, you might like to try a triple whammy of three pieces of fridge philosophy all together:

Be honest with yourself.

Convert a negative thought about somebody (including yourself) or something into a positive one, and forgive.

Focus your attention on the road immediately ahead.

In other words, don't try and pretend it didn't happen, but forgive yourself and get on with living right now instead of in the past.

We live in a culture that doesn't put particular emphasis on the truth. The newspapers and politicians dole out the lies and we tell our fair share too. Would you claim for a little bit more on your insurance than you'd actually had stolen from you? Don't we sometimes say we're unwell in order to get out of something we don't want to do?

It takes courage to tell the truth sometimes. We have to overcome a fear. Our fear is that telling it how it is may create a situation we do not want. Most of the time we imagine that the 'situation we do not want' will be bigger and worse than will be the case – as with me and the 'doghouse story'. I've found that whenever I can find the courage to be straight with people and tell it how it is, without worrying about how I might look, then the consequences are always better than I'd imagined they would be.

Perhaps this is because people aren't stupid, and nobody is expecting you to be perfect. If you do something wrong, then one option is simply to own up and apologise. If the other person won't accept your apology, then that's their problem, not yours, as long as you really meant it in your heart when you gave your apology. If you didn't mean it, then it wouldn't work for *you* anyway, because you weren't being honest with yourself.

In your courageous admission that you are less than perfect, others will even find some comfort – because they know they aren't perfect either. Believe it or not, in the long term people will like you more if you tell the difficult truth, even if they may be disappointed with you in the short term.

However, even if you cannot find the courage to tell the truth to someone else, it is *absolutely vital* that you find the courage to tell the truth to yourself. Denying the truth to yourself will lead you into sadness. Don't be hard on yourself. Forgive others, forgive yourself and, most importantly, forgive me for having made you suffer the doghouse story.

THE FINALE

The next day was a bank holiday Monday. If it had been a Sunday, I might have gone to confession. After all, I had something to confess now, praise the Lord.

'Father, forgive me, but last night I slept with a girl in a doghouse, in full view of a fridge.'

I wonder how many Hail Marys you'd get for that. It probably wasn't on their Sin–Penance guideline chart.

As a matter of fact, any confession I might make would have to begin with the words: 'Forgive me, Father, for I'm not actually a Catholic.'

That was definitely not on the Sin–Penance chart.

After the emotional highs of a short ceremony over-seen by Butch, in which Karen coughed up her 16p and we all taped the coins to the side of the fridge, I began to feel exceptionally tired. My dwindling energy levels needed to be replenished by the calories a cooked breakfast could provide, so I walked down to a café on the Quays that Butch had recommended. As I tucked into my scrambled egg, the truth dawned on me that my journey was almost over, and Dublin was only a few hours' drive away. Feelings of both relief and sadness were overtaken by concern. I might only be a day away from a huge anticlimax.

Up until now, the policy of 'just seeing what happens' had served me well, but now there was a definite case for forward planning. I felt strongly that the finale to such an epic journey required some ceremonial commemoration, and by the time I had finished my breakfast I knew what had to be done.

I ordered a second pot of tea and called the office of *The Gerry Ryan Show*, and outlined my idea. They loved it.

'We'll call you back in ten minutes, Tony,' said Willy, one of the show's producers. 'This is worth interrupting our bank holiday special for. We'll work out exactly how you should do it and then get you to talk about it to Gerry on air. We'll have you on as the first item tomorrow morning too, just to give the thing a big build-up.'

Just the response I was looking for.

Gerry waxed lyrical, as ever.

'I have on the line, Tony Hawks, the Fridge Man, who on his journey round this fair isle has been taken into the hearts of the Irish people, and he has been showered with the kind of hospitality normally saved for a national hero, and he's sunk a bevy or two along the way too. How are you this morning, Tony?'

'Oh, I'm fine, Gerry.'

'I believe that you are about to complete your epic journey. Well done. Congratulations to you. Now, how do you intend to round off a trip like this?'

'Well, I want to march into Dublin with my fridge and I want people to join me as I go.'

'Good idea, a kind of triumphal entry.'

'Exactly.'

'Well, you know Caesar never brought his legions into Rome, but I think on this occasion we can make an exception – you can bring the fridge into Dublin.'

'And I thought it would be a good idea if people joined me on this march with a domestic appliance of their choice.'

'Even better idea. Some friends for the fridge.'

'Exactly, because it's not just about fridges, this, so bring a kettle, a toaster or whatever, because there are all kinds of appliances which need liberating from the confines of the kitchen.'

'You heard him, folks. The man is talking sense, so unplug your kitchen or domestic appliances and join Tony on the march tomorrow, be it with a kettle, a toaster, an iron – or even a cooker, a fridge freezer or microwave.'

A microwave. I should have done my journey with a microwave – I could have done it in a third of the time.

'Now, Tony, listen closely whilst I outline the planned route for this march,' continued Gerry. 'We want people to join you with a kitchen appliance of their choice at Connolly Station at 11 a.m., and having gathered there with food mixers, spatulas or whatever, the procession will then move, in triumph, up Talbot Street, up Henry Street, and then into the ILAC Centre in May Street, where we will have an extravaganza beyond imagination awaiting you there, for you finally to lay this whole trip to rest. So come on, everyone – we want to make Tony's entrance into the capital city a spectacular Disneyesque-style Roman entrance; we want him to be borne, if not on a real chariot then at least on one in the imaginations of the Irish people. Tony, you rest up now and I'll talk to you tomorrow.'

Good. That was a bit of a result. One phone call over breakfast and the country was being mobilised in my support. It was going to be difficult to readjust to life back in London.

'd managed to get myself into a situation that was
wholly inappropriate for the pursuit of hitch-hiking.
I was breaking one of the fundamental rules in that I
needed to be somewhere by a certain time. Leaving at
first light from Wexford should have given me ample
time to be in Dublin by 11 a.m. when *The Gerry Ryan
Show* went live, reporting on me and the fridge and our
Triumphal Entry into Dublin.

Unfortunately, things didn't go according to plan, as
my first car of the day broke down on me. Gerry didn't
panic, but there was a slightly concerned voice when I
spoke to him on air, from a callbox near Ballycanew
just after 9 a.m.

'Goodness, if you don't hurry it up, you won't make
it,' he said. 'Well, if there's anyone in a car, bus or van
anywhere in the vicinity of Ballycanew, then do look
out for Tony and his fridge and speed him on his way
to Dublin. It is, after all, a matter of national importance. We've got to get him to Connolly Station for
eleven o'clock so you can join him with your chosen
domestic appliance, in the triumphal procession to the
ILAC Centre. Obviously, Tony, people will be turning
up in their droves, but have you got any last words
which may encourage the undecided to get down there
and show their support?'

'Well, all I can say, Gerry, is that some marches are
for things and some are *against* things, but never has
there been a march for *absolutely nothing*. Now is our
chance to put that right. Grab your toaster and kettle
and discover, like me, how great it feels to devote
yourself to something truly purposeless. By doing
something with absolutely no point to it, we eliminate
the possibility of failure, because in a sense the worse

it may go, then the more it can be considered a success.'

'Absolutely. Very rousingly put, Tony, and not at all confusing. Well, there you have it, good people of Ireland, now is your chance to join a march which will liberate the nothingness and pointlessness in all of us.'

'That's right. Of course we're using the word "nothingness" in its most positive sense here.'

'Naturally. Now, Tony, good luck on the rest of your hitch this morning, and we look forward to talking to you later on. Both our crack reporters, Brenda Donohue and John Farrell, will be giving us a detailed word picture of exactly what's happening during the triumphant march and the ensuing celebration in the ILAC Centre. It's going to be quite an event, and remember to get yourselves down there because this is the time to make your domestic appliance count. Tony, good morning.'

'Good morning, Gerry.'

When I emerged from the callbox, a lorry immediately drew up alongside me and the driver wound down his window.

'I just heard you on the radio there. If you wait here for twenty minutes I'll be back and I'll take you as far as Arklow.'

And he was gone.

I had no reason to doubt that he'd be back, but I couldn't afford the luxury of twenty minutes, and if I could get a lift before, then I would have to take it.

While hitching, I tried to think of chants that I and my fellow marchers could shout as we strode proudly through Dublin. I came up with a few, but my favourite was one I would have to teach the crowd on my arrival.

TONY: What do we want?
CROWD: We don't know!
TONY: When do we want it?
CROWD: Whenever!

It seemed to strike the right chord.

Kevin and Elaine beat the lorry driver to me. They had heard the interview and made a small detour specially, and since they too were going as far as Arklow, I jumped into their small van and we sped northwards. They were a young couple, both about twenty, and probably the youngest of all those who had stopped for me.

'If I phone ahead, Elaine's mother will cook us all breakfast in Courtown Harbour,' said Kevin.

'I'd love to, really, but I'm running late.'

'That's a shame, because she does a fine breakfast.'

Just beyond Arklow I was back hitching again. I looked at my watch and saw that it was 9.45 a.m. Meeting my deadline was still possible, but a long wait here and *The Gerry Ryan Show* would need to hastily rethink its last hour.

A red car pulled up, and I ran forward to address the driver.

'Where are you headed?' I asked.

'Dublin,' came the magical reply.

I was cutting it fine, but it was all still on.

Peter was unemployed at the moment and on his way to visit friends in Dublin. Not long since a student, he still seemed comfortable with a way of life that was extremely relaxed and laid back. Unfortunately, one area where this manifested itself was in his driving. What should have been a horn-honking, tyre-screeching, risk-taking charge into Dublin was a casual Sunday afternoon tootle into town. All we needed to complete the picture was a tartan blanket on the back seat and a tin of boiled sweets.

Because I was spending most of my time looking at my watch and checking how many kilometres were left before we hit Dublin, I failed to focus on the sadness of the occasion. Peter was my last lift. This was it, the hitch-hiking was over. No longer was I to spread myself by a roadside and put myself at the mercy of a nation's drivers. I would miss it.

Well, bits of it, anyway.

'I could drop you at Sydney Parade Dart Station; my friends don't live far from there. It'll be quicker than suffering the city centre traffic anyway,' said Peter.

'And do you think I'll make it to Connolly Station for eleven?'

'Oh, I'm sure you'll be fine.'

Why do people do that? Say '*I'm sure*' when they're not sure at all? So often people say 'Oh, I'm sure you'll be fine' as a means of preventing further dialogue on the subject:

'I've got to make this speech to a group of feminists about the importance of women staying in the home, and I'm a bit worried about how it might go down.'

'Oh, I'm sure you'll be fine.'

Pete, though, was right. I was fine. I made it just in time to meet with John Farrell, Gerry's roving reporter on the ground, and Christy, a septuagenarian bagpipe player the radio show had booked to add atmosphere. John was carrying a mop, which he claimed was his 'domestic appliance' for the march. However, there were no crowds.

'There's no one here,' I said to John. 'Are you sure we're in the right place?'

'We're in the right place all right. These things tend to kick off slowly.'

He'd done this before? He went on: 'When you start it, then everyone sort of finds it and gets involved. Have you got a radio Walkman with headphones?'

'I have.'

'Well, put it on, and listen. Gerry is just setting the whole thing up now, and if we cross over there to that callbox, I'll give him my first report. Keep listening because I may put you on to him at any point.'

As we crossed the disappointingly uncrowded street, I put on my headphones and couldn't believe what I was hearing. Dramatic music, in fact the soundtrack from *Ben Hur*, was building to a climax. Then Gerry Ryan's voice cut across it, in a sensational and melodramatic tone.

'He came across the pond, the young man and his fridge travelling over land and sea searching for a meaning and purpose in their lives. We speak of Tony Hawks, the Fridge Man. Tony Hawks who came to live amongst us for all but a short while, a messiah of sorts. We felt ourselves not worthy to touch the hem of his fridge, but then we realised that he was but an ordinary man, his fridge but a little fridge, the son of a bigger fridge – the Big Fridge – the huge, gigantic Fridge in the Sky.'

My, he was certainly going for it.

'He travelled the length and breadth of our nation – he became part of our lives. We received Tony Hawks and his fridge into our hearts. Today is the end of his fruitful odyssey.'

His tone now changed and the epic music faded as he tried for the first live link-up.

'Brenda Donohue is in the ILAC Centre in Dublin,

wondering where Tony and his fridge are. How is your wondering, Brenda?'

'Good morning to you, Gerry Ryan. We have a big crowd here just by the fountain at the ILAC Centre and we are awaiting the arrival of Tony Hawks. This is his final destination, this is his final port of call, and people have turned up from all over the country and I have to say that the atmosphere this morning is one of high expectation. You know that feeling of calm before the storm, there's tension in the air, there's longing, there's expectation – we can't wait to see him, we're curious about what he and his fridge look like. We have Mrs Burn who has come all the way from Drogheda, I am surrounded by the women of the Portobello School of Childcare who've all turned up with some domestic appliances, and not just that, they have a chant for Tony, so if he's listening, if he's making his way to the ILAC Centre here in Dublin, we have a chant for you, Tony. On the count of three, tell Tony what you want to say to him. 1 … 2 … 3 … GO TONY GO TONY GO TONY GO! GO TONY GO TONY GO TONY GO!

This was all unbelievable. What was happening at the procession's point of destination was in stark contrast to the scene at its inception. Where I was, there was no real feeling of 'calm before a storm', more a worry that not even a light breeze was on its way.

Meanwhile, back on national radio, Gerry Ryan responded passionately to the girls' chant.

'Isn't that wonderful! If I was Tony Hawks, and I was standing beside my little fridge outside Connolly Street ready to make my triumphant entry into Dublin, then that would touch my heart.'

Well, I was. And it did.

John started waving to me from inside the callbox

where he was waiting with the receiver to his ear. On air, in my headphones I heard the reason why, from Gerry himself.

'We now make our way to Connolly Station in Dublin where John Farrell, our reporter on the ground, is with Tony. John?'

From the callbox, John gave me the thumbs up. How was he going to deal with this situation? Compared to what was happening at the ILAC Centre, in fact compared to anything anywhere, our march was an abject failure. How would John handle this? I soon found out.

'Oh, Gerry,' he said, almost with a tremor in his voice, 'I'm so excited. This man has been going all over Ireland for the last three weeks and two days and he has made a profound impression wherever he has gone. I came here today with my humble kitchen mop and my ice tray, so I am a man prepared. Although, having said that, nothing could have prepared me for meeting the Fridge Man. First of all I should tell you that he has a tan which makes him look like he has been camping in the outback of Australia for the last three weeks. It's amazing. His fridge has been autographed by hundreds of people who are wishing him well and saying how much they enjoy and love his fridge, and now his fridge has come home. We have a bagpiper here, Christy Riley is here to welcome him and I think in the background you can hear him starting to play again …'

John had clearly French-kissed the Blarney Stone. I looked into the callbox and saw John frantically signalling to Christy to start playing.

'… Christy has been entertaining the crowd here with his bagpipes for the last hour or so – ah, there he goes! It's a very loud, full sound, Gerry, and it's drawing lots of attention. We're about to start our procession, but I thought maybe first you'd like to have a word with Tony.'

It was my turn now to be waved at frantically. I moved forward and took the receiver as John handed it to me.

'Tony, how are you?' asked Gerry. 'Is the excitement mounting?'

'Gerry, it's at a fever pitch here. I can't tell you the excitement there is around the place.'

What the hell, I thought, I might as well play ball. A bit of mythologising never hurt anyone. Well, maybe it did sometimes, but I didn't have time for that now.

'I don't think I've ever seen a people like it,' I suggested. 'I have captured the hearts of the Irish people, no question. I am overwhelmed by the response here.'

'I think it now behoves us to prepare for you to continue on your triumphant march,' announced Gerry, silkily leading the show into a commercial break. 'Caesar enters Rome, ladies and gentlemen.'

And so the march began. It wasn't the exact scene I had pictured in my mind's eye over breakfast in Wexford the previous morning. By now, though, my initial disappointment had subsided and I was beginning to draw some perverse satisfaction from this pitiful response to my radio appeals and rallying cries. I had now decided that for a march that was truly pointless, it was entirely fitting that it should be met with such spirited apathy.

I took a moment to observe John, and saw that he wasn't remotely surprised by the lack of numbers on the ground. He had expected as much. I had been naive. Of course, it had been a form of naivety that had borne me so successfully to this point, but this was Dublin, and Dublin was reality. Dublin was to be the big slap round the face. This was a thriving city of commerce, and it was a Tuesday morning just after eleven o'clock. People had work to do, lives to lead, mouths to feed and, thank God, radios to listen to.

Radio listeners were sharing in one of the more spectacular and strangely moving days in their capital's history. There was, however, a substantial gap between the listeners' perception of what was going on and the events that were actually taking place. For those tuned into RTE2 on FM, whether they were in Donegal, Galway or even up in Tory Island, this event was an emotional climax to a touching story, as throngs of well-wishers lined the route, tossing garlands and waving to their hero. For the marcher, just setting off from Connolly Station, it was difficult to view it quite like that. There were three of us. Myself, a roving reporter with a mop, and a pensionable bagpipe player who didn't have the first clue what was going on.

When we reached the ILAC Centre, Brenda and a moderately sized throng cheered me in, and Brenda handed me the microphone and instructed me to make a speech. It would be a speech that would go out live on air and no doubt reach many of the people who had given me lifts and helped me over the previous month. I drew a deep breath.

'Gerry, I can't tell you how moved I am by the response here – there are literally thousands of people, possibly. They go back for – if not for miles, then for yards, well, a number of feet anyway. I just want to pay tribute to the people of Ireland and to the people who have given me lifts along the way. This fridge here is the first fridge to have hitch-hiked round this fair isle of yours. Presumably it won't be the last. I expect there to be a lot of copycat incidences, people taking different domestic appliances out on the road with them, and I'm proud to have opened up that avenue for them. There have been highs on this trip, like taking the fridge surfing in Strandhill, and there have been lows, like when the fridge kept falling off its trolley on the long walk through Galway town centre, but throughout it all there has always been someone on hand with a friendly word and, more often than not, a pint of beer, and for that I just want to say a resounding thank you.'

A warm round of applause greeted my words. Gerry wound things up.

'Well, it only remains for us to complete this odyssey with a special ceremony. Brenda has with her *The Gerry Ryan Show* fridge magnet mayoral chain of office to bestow on Tony, complete with a selection of fridge magnets specially sewn on. Brenda, over to you.'

'Tony,' announced Brenda formally, 'Ireland now pronounces you its Fridge Man.'

The crowd cheered, the music from *Ben Hur* reached its crescendo, and I bowed before Brenda like a victorious Olympic athlete as she placed the mayoral ribbon round my neck. I looked out at the unlikely scene before me and waved to the smiling and laughing onlookers with genuine affection and gratitude.

To my surprise, a tear was rolling down one cheek.

It had been a case of the emperor's new clothes. Once the radio broadcast was over, so too was the fantasy that had sustained it. All of a sudden the Fridge Man felt rather ordinary. The feeling of triumph disappeared into the ether as quickly as the airwaves. It had been great fun, a bit of a laugh all right, but it had all been a bit silly and now the silliness was over. The crowd dispersed almost immediately. People had meetings to attend, jobs to go back to, children to collect from school. No one could afford the time that had been granted to me on the rest of my travels. City life didn't permit such obeisance to whimsy.

The finale might have been fakery, but everything that had preceded it had not. For me this was real. The journey may not have changed the lives of the people of Ireland, but it had changed mine. I was a different, a better, person. I had made discoveries, learned some important lessons. From this day forth I was going to stop for hitch-hikers, laugh along with happy drunks in pubs, and respect the right of the bad guitarist to play along with the rest. I had learned tolerance, I had learned that you could trust in your fellow man for help, and I had learned a new and pleasurable way of acquiring splinters.

If I had been joined by a huge crowd for my Triumphal Entry, then it would have been marvellous, but in an odd kind of way it had been just as good with virtually no one showing up. Somehow it fitted better with the whole ridiculous nature of this bizarre adventure. The fridge journey was an act of brazen silliness, so why not have a ridiculous finale to it?

Perhaps the ridiculousness of the final Triumphal Entry had taught me the most important lesson of all:

Don't take it all so seriously.

We attach so much importance to our lives – because it feels like that's all there is. Is there more? Who knows? Perhaps there's an afterlife, maybe not. Perhaps our bodies die and our spirits live on, maybe not. I just don't know. What I *do* know is that the more importance we attach to our life, then the harder it is for us to enjoy it. If we can keep a sense of perspective about everything, learn to shrug, have a laugh and keep a sense of humour, then think how much easier it could all be.

Perhaps *'Don't take it all so seriously'* sounds flippant, irresponsible even, but take a moment to think about it. It reminds us that we're not as important as we think we are. In terms of the size of the universe, we have no more significance than a tiny ant or buzzing fly. Do we mourn or feel any regret if we kill a fly, a spider or an ant? Most of us don't because we don't consider them to be *important*. Arrogantly, we assume that *we* are.

Well, perhaps we are important. Maybe what we've forgotten, though, is that *everything* is important and that we are no more important than any*one* or any*thing* else. And if everything is important, then it must be the case that nothing stands out above the rest, and so it must also be the case that, conversely, nothing is important.

Have you ever taken a long flight somewhere and flown over lots of different countries at night, looking down at the cities below with all the lights flickering in the houses? They seem like dots in a giant model world strewn beneath us. Millions of people living different lives in different worlds, and yet each one of them wrapped up in their reality, their everyday struggle for happiness, just as we are wrapped up in ours. It's humbling to think that my desire to buy a car, pass an exam, get a job, make up with an estranged lover, have a child, find a lost dog, win a football match or

complete a list, are all replicated by these millions of people who are currently reduced to dots on a landscape. How many of them are taking it all too seriously?

Since my fridge journey, I've genuinely tried to hold on to the lightness of being that came about as a result of the silliness of it all. There seems to be some benefit in not allowing our lives to become too entangled with weightiness, pride and the feeling that everything is of great consequence. Given the choice, I'd rather go with a shrug and smile than head in hands and furrowed brow.

Life is only 'stuff happening'. You're fridge-hiking. Recognising it as that might just make it easier to deal with.

Because every moment that you're unhappy is a waste of you.